MW01137084

Gentling
the Bull

Gentling *the* Bull

The Ten Bull Pictures
A Spiritual Journey

Comments taken from talks by The Venerable Myokyo-ni

 Charles E. Tuttle Co., Inc.
Boston • Rutland, Vermont • Tokyo

Published in Association with The Zen Centre, London

First published in 1996 by Charles E. Tuttle Co., Inc.
of Rutland, Vermont, and Tokyo, Japan, with editorial offices at
153 Milk Street, Boston, Massachusetts 02109.

This edition is a facsimile of an edition first published by the
Zen Centre, London, in 1988.

Library of Congress Cataloging-in-Publication Data

Myokyo-ni.
    Gentling the bull : the ten bull pictures : a spiritual journey /
by Myokyo-ni (Irmgard Schloegl).
        p. cm.
    ISBN 0-8048-3088-6
    1. K'uo-an, 12th cent. Shih niu t'u sung. 2. Spiritual life—Zen
Buddhism. I. Title.
BQ9288.K863M96 1996
294.3'443—dc20   96-6391
                                              CIP

The Ten Ox-Herding Pictures reproduced here are by Shubun (15th century) and are
from the collection of the Shokoku-ji monastery, Kyoto, Japan.

1 3 5 7 9 10 8 6 4 2

Printed in the United States of America

CONTENTS

Introduction

This series of ten pictures is by the 15th century Japanese Zen monk Shubun, but is traditionally attributed to Kakuan, a 12th century Chinese Zen master of the Rinzai lineage. Shubun's pictures are said to be exact copies of the now lost series by Kakuan. The pictures are always presented together with a general Foreword to the series, and individual Prefaces to each picture, by Chi-yuan, a monk in the direct line of Kakuan, and with a set of three poems each by a different author, the first poem being by Kakuan. The pictures themselves are preserved in Shokoku-ji monastery in Kyoto, where Shubun was a monk.

From of old, these pictures have been a favourite training analogy, and are still used as that by present-day Zen masters. The Shubun pictures here reproduced, illustrate accurately and in detail the way of training, and, as Chi-yuan says in his Foreword, they contain 'deeply hidden subtleties'. These latter are conspicuous by their absence in all modern renderings. Such imitations lack the 'teaching details' and thus the flavour and guidelines of the traditional sets.

Foreword, prefaces, and the three sets of poems have been translated from the original Chinese text. The commentary seeks to address not only the student in training, but would like to acquaint the interested reader with what Zen training is fundamentally about, and what it entails. The comments are collected from a series of talks at the 1985 Summer School of the Buddhist Society.

Although the traditional title is 'The Ten Bull Pictures', they have become known in the West as 'Ox-Herding Pictures'. The best known and authoritative are, in English, a partial translation by D.T. Suzuki (Manual of Zen Buddhism, Rider) and in German, a complete translation, with comments by Master Otsu, and by Tsujimura-Buchner; both reproduce the Shubun pictures as essential to the text. The German work is invaluable as the comments are a complete guide through Zen training. An English translation by M. Trevor was published in Japan but has been long out of print. A new translation of the second, revised and enlarged German edition is now in progress.

'Bull' rather than 'ox' seems to fit the meaning. An ox is not difficult to tame, or to herd; he is a peaceful and patient beast of burden, docile, hard-working, obedient — but not so a bull. If met alone in a meadow, it is wiser to quickly get over the fence to the other side. True, the bull might take no notice, but one cannot know — he is unpredictable and dangerous, faster and stronger than I! Do we talk of bull-fighting or ox-fighting?

For easy reference, the names of well-known Zen masters are also given in their Japanese pronunciation [square brackets].

Particular thanks are due to Peter le Marchand who typed out the recorded talks, and patiently re-typed the revised version with all alterations and additions. Thanks also go to John Swain for the lay-out and seeing it through the press.

Foreword

Chi-Yuan wrote
this Foreword to
Master Kuo-an's [Kakuan]
Ten Bull Pictures

The real source of all the Buddhas is the original nature of sentient beings. Through delusion we fall into the Three Worlds, through awakening we suddenly leap free of the Four Modes of Being. Therefore there is something for the Buddhas to do and something for people to carry out. In compassion the old sage set up various ways to teach his disciples sometimes the complete and sometimes the partial truth, leading them suddenly or gradually from the shallow to the profound, from the coarse to the subtle. Finally one of his disciples responded with a smile. He was foremost in the practice of letting go, with eyes like blue lotus. Since then the treasure of the true Dharma Eye has spread everywhere, and has reached even our country.

One who has attained to the core of this truth soars without trace like a bird above all laws and norms. But one attached to the manifold things is caught in speech and misled by words; he is like the clever turtle that tried to wipe out its footprints with its tail — thus making them more conspicuous.

Long ago, Master Ching-chu [Seikyo], aware of the different abilities of sentient beings, adjusted his teachings to the capacities of his disciples and prescribed remedies according to their respective illnesses. To this purpose he drew pictures of gentling a bull. In these, with the bull becoming gradually white, he shows first the growing development of the disciple, and then, at the stage of the spotless purity of the bull, how the ability of the trainee has ripened. Finally, with both man and bull vanished, he illustrates the forgetting of heart and surroundings [I and things].

Though at this stage insight has already pierced through to the root, within the surrounding circumstances something remains that is not yet clear. Here those of shallow root ability tend to fall into erroneous doubt, while students whose understanding is as yet only small or medium, become bewildered and wonder whether they have fallen into empty emptiness, or conversely whether they have been snared by the view of seeming eternalism.

Kuo-an [Kakuan] also composed a poem for each picture. Like Master Ching-chu [Seikyo] before him, he put his whole heart into the execution of these drawings. The ten beautiful poems both shine into and are reflected by each other.

Kuo-an's [Kakuan] Bull Pictures start with the missing of the bull and lead to the return into the origin. These poems fit the differing abilities and needs of those in training like food and drink appease hunger and thirst. With them as guides, I, Chi-yuan, have probed into the profound meaning and extracted hidden subtleties — like a jelly-fish lends its eye to the little shrimps that shelter beneath it.

From 'Searching for the Bull' to 'Entering the Market Place', like attempting to draw a square circle, my prefaces try to describe the indescribable, thus needlessly disturbing the peace of men. There is no heart to look for, even less so a bull! How strange the one who here enters the market place! Unless the heart of the ancient masters has been matched in its very depth, the resulting wrong will spread to the successors. Truly my own Foreword has come from the depth of my heart.

THE BULL PICTURES

Before we can start looking at the Bull-Herding Pictures, we have to acquaint ourselves somewhat with the landscape in which we meet that bull. In style, our commentary will follow the traditional usage, with frequent references to the actual text, and also some repetitions, or some analogies being taken up again at other stages, so as to illustrate different aspects, and developments in depth and subtlety.

Now, the landscape in which this bull roams about is that of the Buddhist teachings, specifically that of the Mahayana.

The real source of all the Buddhas is the original nature that is inherent in all of us, indeed is in everything that lives and passes away. It is in all the changing, impermanent forms that come to be, exist for a while, and then cease to be. This applies not only to sentient beings; Buddha-Nature is also in a chair, a table, in a spoon or in a tree or flower. And since this true nature of all that is is also the real source of all the Buddhas, it follows that the real source of us is not different from that of all the Buddhas. But, 'Through delusion we are sunk in the Three Worlds': only 'by awakening we suddenly leap free of the Four Modes of Being'.

With this, we are right in the midst of the Buddhist

landscape. What are the Three Worlds? We find them referred to again and again in the Buddhist texts; they are the worlds of desire, of form and the formless realm. In these three worlds everything that exists has come to be, changes, and sooner or later ceases to exist again — which means goes into transformation on the Wheel of Change with its six states. This Wheel of Change is also seen as the Wheel of Becoming, or the Wheel of Life (as we see it) and is an abode of suffering, ever continuing and renewing itself. Release from this continuous round of woe, deliverance from the Wheel, is what the Buddhist strives for. Or at least he is hoping by a 'good life' to be reborn in the three happier states.

So because of delusion, through error, we have sunk into these Three Worlds; in them existence, though occasionally also pleasant, is mainly fraught with suffering. Though our true nature is not bound by these Three Worlds and is also free of suffering, through error — 'sticky attachments' — we have fallen into them and so are subject to suffering, conflicts, strife, unhappiness and all kinds of problems. For who has not got any of these?

By awakening, we suddenly spring out of the Four Modes of Being. In Buddhist teaching, these Four Modes of Being (of all that exists) are, respectively, from the womb, from the egg, from moisture, and through transformation (on the Wheel of Change). Thus the Three Worlds and the Wheel with its six states constitute the Buddhist stage on which the whole play takes place. The Buddhist feels oppressed by the prospect of endlessly revolving on that Wheel, of having to undergo the same old round of suffering caused by delusion, longs for release from it, and to awaken to the true nature, to what we really are.

The Four Modes of Being, then, state the conditions for coming to be, the means by which everything that has existence originates. Womb and egg are obvious, though moisture may be somewhat puzzling. One has only to be in a tropical country during the wet season to see a little puddle in one day become all green and wriggling with life. Through transformation — apart from the 'formless realm' — we may take it as the karmic circling on the Wheel of Change, of becoming in Samsara, which is this our world with its unsatisfactoriness or suffering. Sentient beings whirl interminably on this Wheel, bobbing up and down in the sea of birth and death without respite. The six states on the Wheel are that of heavenly beings, to be thought of as 'manifest' spiritual forces rather than 'gods' of popular imagination; then the realm of the fighting demons, that of the hungry ghosts, that of beings in the miserable states or hells, that of animals and finally that of human beings. None of these states is permanent; the length of stay in them is karmically conditioned which means we ourselves are the arbiters of our 'fate' because our actions and reactions determine the duration as well as the destination. Through these states we pass again and again — often this is taken as meaning from one life to another. We leave that for we do not know. But certainly we pass through these states umpteen times a day and so are well acquainted with our transmigrations through them. On waking up in the morning, 'Oh, I wish I did not have to get up'; and we are in one of the miserable states, among miserable beings. Then at breakfast my egg is not boiled as I like it and I have a row with the wife — and so am shunted among the fighting demons. Then I miss the bus and 'Oh, if only transport would be better, if only I could have a car, if only there would be parking at work, if only . . .' and that is the realm of the hungry ghosts. Occasionally in the course of the day we also migrate through the human state, fleetingly. It is quite a rare state for us to be in for any length of time, though we all have human bodies.

In Buddhism it is said that deliverance from the Wheel is possible only from the human state. It is said that this ever revolving Wheel is kept in motion by the Three Fires, which are first, greed, desire, ceaseless, desperate wanting; second, hot anger; and third, delusion. Now, considering the billions of sentient beings alone, it is a rare chance to be born with a human body. A traditional analogy describes how rare such a chance is: in the world ocean floats a board with a hole in the middle. Also in that ocean lives a blind turtle, and once every hundred years it needs to surface for a breath of air. If it should so happen that on surfacing it puts its head right through the hole in that board, that surely is a very remote chance. Just as rare is it to be born with a human body.

Even though we now have that extremely rare boon, a human body, we are not yet inhabitants of the human state, but transmigrate daily through all the states on the Wheel, and so only for short periods of the day are we truly human. Yet deliverance from the Wheel is possible only from the human state. So our first and most important task is to labour to become human beings, residents of the human state, not just temporary visitors, homeless vagrants traversing it as well as all the other states.

Traditional Zen training is thus concerned first with becoming truly human, that is, able to act, feel, speak and think in a truly human way; in short to be truly human, which means to remain so under all circumstances, good, bad or indifferent. It is natural and easy for us to be fully human in the rare moments when everything goes just as I like it; we are then at our best: kind, forgiving, tolerant, helpful, ready to be there or give a helping hand, happy. But when somebody accidentally treads on my toe, what then? Something erupts in that good, kind being, flares wild and primitive — and that something is not just the pain!

We stand in need of training because of this propensity. That which snorts up in me at the moment I am thwarted, or my will is crossed, and of which normally I am not even aware, that is what in our analogy is called the bull — the wild aspect of our heart which is also the human heart, and which we share with all human beings.

To think of this bull as an enemy is the greatest mistake we can make. True, to begin with we would like to be rid of this bull. Fortunately this is not possible, for the bull stands for that tremendous life energy which is not mine but is the true nature which is also the source of all the Buddhas and of all that exists. That, surely, cannot be said to be my energy or strength. It is of a power that far exceeds what I can muster in cold blood. I am usually quite unaware of it, or conversely may fear its power.

The northern tradition of Buddhism holds that 'the passions are the Buddha-Nature' and vice versa — which statement concerns the energy itself; it flares as 'my' reactions, but in the absence of 'I' reverts to what it always has been. This will be discussed in more detail at a later stage.

The saying that the passions are the Buddha-Nature must never be understood to indicate that I can now let it rip in all directions, and thus exhibit my Buddha-Nature. While I think of it as mine, while I am still there, the bull will always carry me away.

Who has never experienced any uprush of bull-energy, or has never been carried away by the bull? This power, in its manifestation as bull, is a very deceptive force, and so we need to be quite clear about it. First and foremost, it is not my bull. When we look for him, seemingly he is not there. Arisen in all his magnificent power (a firework of passion!), he rather has me. Once again, he is not the enemy, for the passions are the Buddha-Nature — it is the same energy that flares wild in the one and in-forms the form in the other. How so?

The Three Signs of Being are the foundation of all the Buddha's teachings: change, suffering or unsatisfactoriness, and No-I. 'Subject to change are all compounded things'; well, yes, we know. But when the change goes from what I like to what I do not like, or means parting from what I love and being thrown together with what I loathe — this is a cause of suffering and yet is our common human lot. The sufferer is 'I', that imaginary being concocted from picking and choosing. Sosan, the third Chinese patriarch, started his great poem 'On Faith in the Heart' with the statement, 'The Great Way is not difficult, it only avoids picking and choosing'. Yet, when we look carefully, the very nature of 'I' is picking and choosing — 'I' would like this, do not want that; the floor should be polished; not orange juice, I wanted lemon juice; the sun is shining, the garden is getting too dry, it ought to rain! Why can't I meditate single-mindedly without any distracting thoughts? Whatever thus goes through our mind, good, bad or indifferent, is all picking and choosing. It is a vicious circle, for if I now want to stop and get rid of picking and choosing, that, too, is picking and choosing! I am caught in it, the Wheel of Samsara! The Buddha showed the Way of deliverance from that Wheel — only his way is very different from what I imagine.

Because picking and choosing goes on continuously, we deludedly assume a something or somebody who does it; we then call this hypothetical doer 'I' and take it for real! Actually there is no such thing as I, only the continuous stream of picking and choosing. By following the Buddha's Way, by undertaking a traditional training, this stream of picking and choosing begins to lose its compulsion and gradually evens out. The difference between the one and the other is very clear. It would be nice to have a cup of coffee now if possible, but if not, that is all right too. Or, I must have a cup of coffee now to steady myself or I cannot carry on! The end of picking and choosing is not, repeat not, ceasing from all picking and choosing as I mistakenly assume; as long as there is a body, there is picking and choosing — the very way I walk is as suits this body best; no harm in that, is there? But the compulsion, the heat, the Fire, the intensity of 'I must' (have or get rid) is what afflicts, what causes suffering and problems.

Hence the gentling of this intensity or energy is the Buddha's Way out of suffering.

Seen from that point of view, it is I who am the maker of all my problems and the arbiter of my suffering. The Buddha's great teaching of No-I, therefore, warns against taking things personally and shows the way things really are. That is not to say they are all the same. Flowers are red and yellow and white; but it is not a question that white flowers are better than red ones. And trees are green. All things are the way they really are, and this way applies equally to red and white flowers, and to green trees; they come to be, they exist for a time, and they cease to be — this is the way of all forms, all that exists. Such seeing, which is Buddha-seeing, genuine insight, is not possible for 'me' because of picking and choosing and thus being partial. Or, to put it concretely, because of my taking sides selfishly and hence becoming 'fired'. Without any training, I cannot help this bias because of the delusion that I am the one who picks and chooses, rather than a neutral stream of picking and choosing within a situation — as water flows, or the sun shines.

So what is needed is the cultivation of a different type of seeing, because as long as the notion of I is present, there will always be something that I do not like. On such an encounter, the energy rises or rushes up seemingly of its own accord; it either swamps me, overwhelms and carries me away — or I manage to refuse it and hold it at bay. Either way, energy flaring up as the Fires is the consequence of my picking and choosing. In the absence of I, and so without this intentional, biased, hence heated, hence Karma-producing, picking and choosing, the energy is just what it is and always has been, the Buddha-Nature. As that, it is and acts in all that is, in-forms all forms — a cat will act as cats do, and a bird as a bird. We, deluded human beings, are out of that harmony — is that perhaps the biblical story of the Fall and consequently being driven out of paradise? Yet a fish in the water does not know he is in it, for it is his natural element — he acts in conformity with it and his surroundings. As an analogy, this cannot be taken too far, but may give a hint, especially when coupled with an old Zen saying that to begin with, trees are seen as trees and water as water; then trees are no longer trees, and water not water (the split state); and in the end trees are again seen as trees, and water as water. Master Rinzai says of a liberated being that he is and acts 'as lively as a fish playfully leaping in the water' — utterly at home and happy! The quiet sea carries a good swimmer; he need not strain.

This in-born in-form-ation, the 'naturally knowing' which is Not-I, is the Buddha-Nature inherent in all beings. In us human beings it is overlaid, obscured and misinterpreted by my biased partiality. Consequently, the energy, constellated, is itself blinded and erupts impulsively, hot and compelling — quite out of harmony with the situation, and is thus the source of suffering. Release from suffering, the Buddha's Way, then, depends on the absence of I, the artificial subject of the natural stream of picking and choosing. So, before picking and choosing, before thinking of good and bad, what is the True Face?

This is the turning over which the training helps us to do, and for which there is the beautiful Buddhist analogy of the wave and the ocean. One wave, likened to I, may, as every I does, think itself separate from everything else, apart from (rather than part of) all that is. This is a very exposed and lonely position, is it not? Poor I! Consequently, I am easily frightened, hence cramp up, always on the defensive and therefore by way of over-compensation either aggressive or shrinking in my dealings with the other or the outside. So I have many problems and difficulties; I am rarely at ease.

Coming back to the analogy of the single wave, such an individual wave, isolated from all that is around, would naturally feel itself as separate, exposed, at the mercy of its surroundings which often seem 'threatening'. Just as such a wave rears up on the brink of breaking, interfered with as it is by all the other waves around, if that wave could but realise that whether up, down or any other way, it is nothing but ocean, as indeed are all the other waves also, could fear then have any hold on this our particular wave? Even losing its 'individual' temporary form as a wave and becoming again what it always has been, ocean, can hold no terror, can it? If endowed with consciousness, it would thus once more have become aware of being in-formed by and at-one with, itself, that is its inherent ocean-nature. This, though not mine, is yet inalienable. It in-forms and guides the form — each form according to, or in harmony with, that form, as fits that specific form and the stages of its duration in form. Thus, a mouse will always predictably and in all circumstances do and act as a mouse — not as a cat, nor as an ant. And a puppy will play as a puppy does and not behave like an old dog, and vice versa!

Moreover, with this insight, all the other waves around would be seen as equally nothing but ocean. Could any tension, perturbation or whatever still exist in the presence of such insight?

Even as a mere intellectual exercise, it may be helpful for us to realise not only where the Way points, but also as undermining the fear that is in all of us, in every I, of not having what we need — which at bottom is the fear of plunging out of existence. For, whether frightened of loss or frightened of death or of whatever else we may fear, every I is frightened of something. Fear is the other side of I; these two belong together like head and tail of a coin. Just this is the basic split from which I, we all, suffer.

In Buddhism, delusion is considered to be one of the Three Fires, as well as the first link in the Twelve-Linked Chain of Causation, and hence the prime cause that sets the Wheel in motion and is the prime cause of suffering. This delusion induces consciousness arbitrarily to assume a subject, a doer, for the natural stream of picking and choosing. This has a two-fold consequence, apart from the split into subject and object. First, this arbitrary assumption, I, now invades the stream of picking and choosing and, self-biased, takes sides, attaches to this and loathes that. In this process of self-biased selection, it pitches itself against all that is 'other' and hence, secondly, still under the sway of the same delusion, feels itself separate and alone, hence frightened. Yes, I and fear are inseparable, one being the other side of the other. All imagination, delusion; and the Heart Sutra spells out the cure, 'In the absence of thoughts, what is there to fear?'

Analogous to the wave's becoming aware of its ocean nature, realisation of the true nature or Buddha-Nature delivers from feeling separate, from loneliness, and so from all fear. This constitutes the insight of the Buddha, the insight to which the ascetic Gautama awakened, suddenly, after years of cultivation. From this great insight and its consequent great compassion, he spent the rest of his long life teaching those willing and able to listen — as the scriptures put it, for the 'sake of those whose eyes are but little covered with dust'. Never is this teaching to be rammed down unwilling throats, only to be made available to those willing and eager to learn. But it is also important to realise that it is a teaching to be practised rather than learnt!

This sets the background against which the drama of gentling the bull takes place, for our training analogy. So there is something for Buddhas to do, and for us people there is something we have to carry out. The man who awoke under the Bo-tree and became the Buddha did not settle down in some remote mountain fastness and live out his life quietly and happily without any concern for others. He was available to people who came to him with problems, to seekers, pointing out to them the Way to that insight that had arisen in him, and of which he never said that it was new, but only claimed that he had re-discovered an ancient way leading to an ancient city. He also stressed repeatedly that it was not something that had to be acquired from outside, something to be added, but that, however obscured by attachments, delusion and so on, it was inherently always there and only had to be uncovered. 'In this fathom-long body, oh monks, I declare to you, is the world, the beginning of the world, the end of the world, and the way that leads to the end of the world', and so of its suffering. His message in general was, 'Suffering I teach, and the Way out of suffering'.

As said above, the real source of all the Buddhas is the true nature of all that is, lives and passes away. So that nature, though forgotten, need not be acquired. It has always been there, is always there, and can be re-discovered by suitable means of practice or cultivation. These are specified by the Buddha and derive from his own experience. They spell out the means that led to his awakening and which, if followed correctly and dedicatedly, will open that same insight to us — exactly the same, as it is inherent in its entirety in all of us.

This momentous re-discovery is the adventure that awaits all of us if we endeavour to follow the Buddha's Path. This is done by actually walking it step by step, not by head-learning only, or saying, 'Yes, there is such a Way, and there is such a thing as awakening,' and then arguing about what awakening is and what it is not. Only by actually treading the Path with our own two feet, and thus following it, can we, each individually for ourselves, re-discover that ancient path that leads to the ancient city of the human heart. This is not mine, for we all have it. As Zen students, we recall the words of Bodhidharma, 'directly pointing to the human heart, seeing into its nature and becoming Buddha.' That is the essence of what not only Zen training but all Buddhist training is about.

So for this reason there is something for Buddhas to do. Having re-discovered the true nature that is in all that exists, there is the task — a true labour of love — of making it available;

that is letting it shine and helping others towards it. Thus made accessible, whether others then make use of it and follow it, is up to them. The making it available is what Buddhas have to do. It is said therefore that Buddha is still here training with us, and so is Bodhidharma, showing us the Way.

And for us, the people, there is also something to carry out, such as listening to the teachings if we are so inclined — or reading and studying the teachings if we are sufficiently interested. If so, and they seem meaningful and touch our heart, we ponder them and may feel the aspiration to walk that Way and so start the training. Hence it is said that there are three stages: hearing with the ear (or, as most of us do more reading than listening to lectures, reading with the eye); pondering in the heart; and practice with the body. For us Westerners it is particularly important to realise that the practice is much more physical than mental. Work with the bull is not a mental exercise; we are working with the Fires that flare up in the body. The Fires, or the passions, are traditionally said to be red — the colour also of blood. If we are unwilling — or unprepared — to endure emotional onslaughts, and attempt to train the mind only, we miss the whole import, deceive ourselves and the bull is not even seen, much less gentled.

So for us people in the world, what we have to carry out is to re-discover ourselves, and that means first to find and then to become truly acquainted with the bull. Not that the bull has ever been missing — he is the other house-mate in the human body! But having become estranged from each other, he is now wild, and to catch and truly gentle him is a formidable undertaking. It entails the complete transformation of the unpredictable, wild and stubborn bull-nature to a total gentleness or gentility·that remains truly human under all circumstances, however trying or tempting. As a training analogy, it will engage us all the Way. Little by little drawing a bit closer, we learn to bear the presence of the bull instead of running away as we usually do. And finally the hard, patient, bone-breaking struggle of truly gentling his nature which is also our nature! Hence we must never think of the bull as an enemy. For if we do so, we want to get rid of him. Fortunately we cannot do so for, though primitive and wild, he is also the energy or strength that is needed for the much harder task of gentling and so transforming him. This is what we have to carry out.

Out of 'com-passion' with human suffering, the Buddha taught the Way out of it. That Way he had himself gone, and knew to be effective. He pointed it out, either wholly or partially as the case might demand. Com-passion literally means suffering with; the afflicting passions of the Fires cause our suffering; but the passion of Christ also was suffering, undergone to deliver us, hence also out of com-passion. The Buddhist term *Klesa* is translated here as afflicting passions in preference to the usual defiling passions; for we do suffer from them.

Their eradication (that is the transformation of their inherent energy) is what Buddhism is all about. Indeed, from whichever angle we look at it, it always amounts to the same basic prospect: Way out of suffering = eradication of afflicting passions = transformation of the energy that flares in the passions into the Buddha-Nature = gentling the bull = becoming human = the realisation of No-I = the end of all fear = insight into the nature of change = deliverance = insight into the way all things really are = the end of suffering = awakening. Spelt out like this we see the almost awesome concordance of all the Buddhist teachings, of all schools, all persuasions; truly they speak, though in different tongues, yet with one voice! That is the voice of the Buddha; our training and our understanding need to be checked against it continuously so that it can develop to the magnitude of that overwhelming insight, rather than deviate from the Buddha's Way into 'as I see it', which is both belittling the Buddha's Way and deceptive, not leading out of suffering.

As to the *Klesas*, the afflicting passions, they happen to us. We do not have them in the sense of producing or making them; they are not mine , for by an act of will I can neither make them arise nor lay them down! Though we might claim, 'I have an emotion', the fact is that 'it has me'. It is very important for us to realise this fact. Emotions happen to us: often against our will or reason; they afflict us, we suffer from them.

If for example a wave of real anger flares up in me (the same applies in the case of an overwhelming desire or any other 'irresistible' attraction or repulsion), it has the power to carry me away. Being 'beside myself' I may snap at a friend who then is very upset. Cooled down, I cannot believe I could have said what I did. 'It just slipped out I do not know how. I must have been beside myself'; which is exactly what I was, beside myself because overwhelmed by anger.

If we look at history, in such states of being 'beside myself' we have perpetrated much that does not deserve the adjective human. It is no good unloading this onto 'them'. Neither historically, nor collectively, nor individually, are we irreproach-able, for subject to the passions we all are — if not the cruder ones, certainly to views and opinions — from food fancies to phobias and irrational fears, quite apart from our vaunted religious, political and other opinions. It is a formidable array, is it not? This is the powerful 'field' in which the bull holds sway. Hence the propensity of being gripped and carried away is something with which we had better come to terms. Suffer we do from it, one way or another. How do we feel after a violent row; surely we all recall one? All passion spent, thoroughly exhausted because all the energy has discharged itself! Then we have to wait until the energy reservoir begins to fill itself up again. Meanwhile, we are 'burnt out' for the time being.

Modern 'Release Methods' utilise this discharge syndrome, but if habitually indulged in, it is enervating in the sense that the bearing strength atrophies. Then it goes the same course as any other addiction — release must be sought more and more often, resulting in ever increasing enervation or weakening. For the passions really afflict us; they come over us we do not know how, and usually have carried us away before we had time to think. Come back to ourselves again, we remember little or nothing of what we said or did in the heat of the moment. Language has all the necessary expressions for it! Engaged in an argument, we might proclaim with real conviction and unctuous certainty what we know to be true. If we but had a tape recording of it, to listen to it later in cold blood, it would be a sobering experience indeed! For what in the heat of the moment seemed to be the most lucid truth or clincher was in fact so blatant and banal as to make me blush; and was beside the point as well. It is the Fire, the heat, intensity or power which makes what we think and say in such a state seem lucid and profoundly true. But factually, in such a fired and hence blind state, only the most commonplace can be produced, the inanities of lovers' talks being a classical example; they seem significant because 'blown up' by the intensity of the Fires.

So, afflicted by the passions we often are — whether by the cruder ones of fierce wanting or anger and so on, or by the much subtler and pernicious ones of 'my considered opinions'. What we need to learn now is not to be carried away by the Fires but to put their energy to good use. Energy is dynamic: work it must — hence in Buddhism the distinction between skilful and unskilful. Skilful use of the energy would seem to let it forge a true human being inhabiting the human realm; and from there beckons the truly human task of assisting others to attain to this all-important human state.

But how to set about it? Awareness of such states of being fired, and their consequences, brings first-hand knowledge of the suffering they entail and produce, for oneself and for others.

So from compassion an effort is made to endure the

presence of the Fires rather than being always carried away by them. That is the beginning. Here we are reminded again of our transmigrating on the Wheel of Change. Carried away, we sometimes act like fighting demons, then again behave like hungry ghosts, or suffer without any redress as animals do, or we are in the desperate state as the beings in hell; occasionally we also are wafted up, soaring like heavenly beings and, like these, unaware of suffering all round; and for short periods we are also human! So we go round and round that Wheel. From this awareness arises true compassion, the pity of not being able to stay in the human realm from which only deliverance is possible. To point out the Way towards it is the task of Buddhas, what they have to do. And what we have to carry out is to practise so that we may re-discover that Way for ourselves — and then point it out to others.

The Buddha showed the Way out of suffering. All his diverse teachings are but variations of this basic theme. Our gratitude and admiration and respect go to the Buddha for making them so manifold. For not only on a walk through the park, but in the 'inner landscape' too, one may be inclined to walk along water or by the trees. 'The Dharma-Gates (teachings) are manifold, we vow to learn them all.' In some mysterious concord, if we but truly tread this one way — and we cannot tread more than one at a time — walking along it, all other ways begin to reveal themselves as but one. The treading of the Way is also emptying ourselves out, and consequently all our judgements, opinions, and seeming separateness fall off of themselves.

But it is not easy to tread this Way. When the going gets difficult, if the heart does not truly incline, we give up treading it. Only if the heart inclines can we continue, for this Way leads 'beyond myself'. Thus, though I feel that I cannot go further, the heart's aspiration is itself the strength to pull and carry me on — Not-I.

So in the beginning we have to find that one Buddha Way to

which our heart inclines. Having walked a goodish stretch of it, we begin to see that the other Buddha ways are very much the same, only in somewhat different landscapes. Hence the importance of going one way only. Mixing one's drinks produces a hangover, not because the drinks are necessarily bad but because of the indiscriminate mixing. But once well on the single Way, as when all its tributaries have combined in a mighty river and there is no longer any doubt about its course, the tributaries may then be explored for the sake of others who might incline to them. Hence 'The Dharma-Gates (teachings) are manifold, I vow to study them all.' The Buddha, out of pity and compassion, established all these teachings for the sake of sentient beings — the same truth expressed in various ways, either fully or partially as fitted the capabilities of his audience.

One might be tempted to ask, why not all of it, the whole in one go — why sometimes partially only? There is an old saying which modern Westerners rather resent, 'Do not talk to the frog in the well about the vastness of the great ocean.' I do not feel myself to be a frog in a well and do not like to think of myself as one — it slights me! Besides, not liking it where I am, there must be something more. So I am very interested in this vast ocean, and would like to see, to 'experience' it.

Fortunately this is mostly beyond me — for if it were revealed to me in one go, right here and now, it would terrify me and might even kill me! The sense of awe is no longer known in our spiritual ice-age. Yet in the Bible, too, whenever a heavenly messenger — an angel, for example — addresses a mortal, a human being, he invariably starts with 'Fear not' to bridge the terror of the 'totally other' and establish the possibility of hearing the message.

In our age of enlightenment we have forgotten this sense of awe and wonder, of reverence, of veneration and devotion and humility, have forgotten the folding of the hands and the bowing of the head, the bowing of the heart as well as the body. All this no longer means anything to us who live in our heads only. But we do sense that a whole dimension is missing and the heart longs for it! Seriously considered, how might we feel if suddenly confronted, say in the small hours of the night, by a column of fire of uncanny hue? The above statement of the frog in the well is a most compassionate warning so that I may not become too quickly exposed to that vast emptiness of which Bodhidharma spoke, for it would frighten me out of my wits. All traditions have their warnings against just that. It takes a long time and much hard training, a willing letting go ever a little more, of folding the hands and again giving oneself, laying oneself down, until there is so little left that the vast emptiness of the wide ocean need not be confronted any more because there is no longer an I to confront anything. Again we meet the Buddha's teaching of No-I. This is also where the wave has realized that it is nothing but ocean, or the trainee becomes aware of the 'True Face', the original, true nature of all that is.

These days, sadly, the religious aspect is rarely mentioned, even by Buddhists themselves, because it is considered either not scientific or not within the lines of what is popular. Spiritual arrogance leaves the heart cold and is far from the Way of the Buddha. More important, awareness of the religious aspect is imperative because only then can we begin to realise the very real need for folding the hands, bowing the head and the often stiff neck, and so laying down our burden. In so doing, we find support and consolation in times of sorrow, grief or fear. Moreover, in the act of laying down, the heart may light up with a very first glimpse of its true nature.

All traditions have stories highlighting this. These make us realise that the inner way is the same in all religions. From that we learn to respect the other religious traditions, while being grateful for having found in Buddhism a Way we can walk. We might not have felt inspired to walk in another landscape, as it were.

As to laying down, there is a teaching story in the Hasidic tradition that is very helpful. A truly saintly rabbi had a brilliant student who one day asked, 'How is it that nowadays nobody can see the face of God when in the old days many saw His countenance?' 'My son, because nowadays nobody can stoop so low,' was the reply. We may usefully reflect on this story when once more our back is in the process of stiffening up, 'Here I make my stand. I will not, cannot go further, cannot or will not do or countenance such and such.' Who could stoop so low?

The Buddha taught sometimes a sudden and sometimes a gradual approach — if we cannot yet stoop so low at one go, then possibly we can learn it little by little in a gradual way. What is important is not the learning how to do this, but our actual doing it again and again!

Once the Buddha was to address a large assembly that had come to listen to his Dharma teachings. Somebody handed him a flower. He just sat there, saying nothing, and silently raised up the flower. The whole assembly sat dumb, not knowing what it was about, waiting for him perhaps to comment on the lifting of the flower — everybody picking and choosing and speculating on what was going to come any moment now. But nothing came! One only in that vast audience, Mahakasyapa, seeing the Buddha's lifting up of the flower, smiled. Upon which the Buddha said, 'I have the priceless jewel of the true Dharma-eye, and I now hand it to you, Mahakasyapa!'

This is said to have started the transmission which the Zen school considers itself to be based upon, the transmission from heart to heart from the Buddha through Mahakasyapa and all the generations unbroken until it has come down to our day. In grateful memory it is chanted every morning in Zen temples and monasteries, and the main memorial days are kept to remember gratefully those who spent their lives treading the

Way and transmitting it so that we of today may follow it.

That sets the scene. In the landscape we can now ourselves set out on our search for the heart-bull; with mountains, trees, meadows and swamps, it is the landscape of the Buddhist teachings of the human heart.

I — SEARCHING FOR THE BULL

The search for what? The bull has never been missing. But without knowing it the herdsman estranged himself from himself and so the bull became lost in the dust. The home mountains recede ever further, and suddenly the herdsman finds himself on entangled paths. Lust for gain and fear of loss flare up like a conflagration, and views of right and wrong oppose each other like spears on a battlefield.

POEMS

1

Alone in a vast wilderness, the herdsman searches for his
    bull in the tall grass.

Wide flows the river, far range the mountains, and ever
    deeper into the wilderness goes the path.

Wherever he seeks, he can find no trace, no clue. Exhausted
    and in despair,

As the evening darkens he hears only the crickets in the
    maples.

2

Looking only into the distance, the searching herdsman
    rushes along.

Does he know his feet are already deep in the swampy
    morass?

How often, in the fragrant grasses under the setting sun,

Has he hummed Hsin-feng [Shinpo], the Song of the
    Herdsman, in vain?

3

There are no traces in the origin. Where then to search?

Gone astray, he stumbles about in dense fog and tangled growth.

Though unwitting, grasping the nose of the bull, he already
    returns as a guest,

Yet under the trees by the edge of the water, how sad is
    his song.

Picture 1

SEARCHING FOR THE BULL

The story starts here, and we will have to look very carefully at these pictures. Why the search? Though the bull has never been missing, he seems to be, because the herdsman has turned away from himself. In such turning, we split ourselves into two; then, holding to one side only, we ignore or deny the other side to the point of losing sight of it, forgetting it. Suddenly we become aware that something is missing — we know not what but have an inkling of a whole dimension lacking and long for 'completion'. For somehow in our midriff there seems to be a gaping hole — the source of our insecurity, of our aggression and our wants, of blunders and of fears. Usually we spend our lives in futile attempts to fill this insatiable void; it also makes us gobble up, indiscriminately but enthusiastically, whatever there is about as new means — a new fad, new idea, all food of any description: organic, health, whole, fibrous, raw, mental — anything that promises to fill that empty hole inside. The tragedy is — delusion is one of the Three Fires — that the more hungry we are, the more gullible we become. So, however much we try to gobble down, it does not answer, we still remain hungry. The hungry ghosts perfectly portray this predicament and the suffering it entails.

So the search for the bull is searching for that which cannot be gobbled up because it never was outside, lost or missing. In the preface to his Koan collection, 'The Gateless Gate', Master Mumon says, 'The treasures of the house do not come in by the front gate.' They belong to the house, are there already. Accordingly, what can and does fill that voracious hole is not something that needs to be acquired from outside. And so, fulfilment, in the sense of wholeness, is re-discovering what has never been missing, but of which we have become unaware since we turned away from ourselves. This being turned away from ourselves is also being at loggerheads with ourselves, and as such is that basic delusion (*Avidya*) the Buddha considers to be the first link of the Twelve-Linked Chain of Dependent Origination.

This split or divided state is portrayed in Picture 1. There the herdsman sets out on his quest. He knows there is something missing but does not know what, does not even know that his feet walk in one direction while his head is turned to the other. He is not at one with himself, and so, though he searches desperately, his search does not prosper. Even just to set one foot after the other and keep walking is sometimes very difficult.

I may, for example, have heard a little about Buddhism and now from that develop my own views. I might even take it into my head that meditation is a kind of miraculous cure for all my problems, and if only I meditate long and hard enough, the miracle will happen! This is one of the many aspects of a divided position. We are impatient, quick to judge on the basis of insufficient understanding; and so, unbeknown to ourselves, we are under the sway of hot opinions, that is of the afflicting passions. This is why we get so easily stuck and have so much trouble. For what happens if I move one leg forward, and, on seeing that this 'advances' me, now insist on walking on that 'trusty' leg only instead of walking on both my legs? I soon end up in so split a position that I can no longer move at all! It is a useful analogy to show how ludicrous such hopeful pursuits are. And how futile.

People often become discouraged, even worried or frightened, when attempting to 'meditate' without guidance; but are nevertheless upset when told, 'Well, that is only to be expected; you have done nothing but meditate, and it is practically tearing you apart. Stop for a while and start moving the neglected other leg instead — concentrate on the Daily Life (*Sila*) practice.'

The fact is, we are not too keen on the Daily Life Practice, if we have ever heard of it at all! We prefer to put our hope in so-called meditation, 'just sitting' even if the legs hurt. The Daily Life Practice is bothersome and difficult, and there is no end, for it is all day long. But *Sila* Practice cannot be ignored, for the inner or moral strength that is developed in this practice is essential for any serious attempts at meditation. So the search continues.

Having turned away from himself, the herdsman has become a stranger to himself. He does not know himself any more, though he thinks he does. He has an inkling that something is missing, but knows not what. The 'other part' has become estranged; and though it often drives or even rides him, he is not aware of it.

So the herdsman has lost himself in hazy regions. He is trying to win back to the familiar landscape but the home mountains recede ever further and he suddenly finds himself stuck and entangled. 'Desire for profit and fear of loss flare up like a conflagration.' Both desire and fear are the consequence of the continuous stream of picking and choosing which, when mistaken for I in the sense of I doing the picking and choosing, I being the subject, becomes partial and biased and so splits seeing what is into opposite pairs; thus arise the 'ten thousand things'. But factually there is no such I that does the choosing; it is only assumed.

Having set myself up, so to speak, and with that first act having also created all that is, including gods and devils, I am the one who does: if I am not here, things get scary! With the assumption of an I doing the choosing, there also arise desire for profit and fear of loss. Here is one of the stories related of Master Huang-po [Obaku], Master Rinzai's teacher. The great T'ang emperor was an admirer of his, and one day both stood by the river that went through the capital. The emperor was pleased to see the river crowded with all kinds of craft, and said complacently, 'Ours is indeed a mighty empire — just look at the crowded river.' 'I see but two ships on this river,' said Obaku. 'What can you mean? The river is teeming with ships.' 'Two ships only', firmly repeated Obaku, 'the ship of gain, and the ship of fame.' The emperor took his words to heart, and under his rules and reforms, the great T'ang empire took shape.

If we think in terms of picking and choosing, is there anything except these two ships? Gain, materially or spiritually, to be secure and safe, satisfied — and whatever diminishes and takes away from me evokes fear. Yes, picking and choosing has its roots in our very existence, and we do well to consider it very carefully, because it is connected with I and fear. 'I' may be nothing but a deluded assumption, but as that, none the less real to one thus deluded — as is the concomitant fear. Once awoken from a nightmare, we know it was not real, but it felt very real while it lasted!

Now, traditional training has its built-in ways slowly and safely to undermine this fear. Remember that frog in the well. For setting out on the way to become nothing again, fear is never far away. As I become less preoccupied with myself in the course of training, fear also diminishes, and accordingly changes take place of themselves. Do we realise that it is out of that same fear that views of right and wrong stand up in opposition to each other like spears on a battle-field? That in an argument over perhaps something utterly trivial, our voice suddenly changes and something I do not know is speaking out of me now. Rarely do we realise it when this change overcomes us — only in retrospect or by its effect do we come to know of it. The bull has invaded us once more.

What compels desire for gain and fame with the intensity of a survival value is that 'gaping hole' previously mentioned, and hence the consequent fear of loss that is often so patently out of proportion with the issue in question.

There is a still further turn of that delusory involvement. For now I need to hold up and keep going the delusion of 'I' that set me up in the first place, has assumed I a doer! Thus I must continuously pump energy into it to keep it alive as existing in my opinions, even flaunt it if need be, to be affirmed and appreciated by you — because deep down is always the gnawing doubt-fear that after all I might be no-thing. So I am really something like a blown-up balloon in the shape of a manikin. Seeing it serenely floating up there, ah! that's me all right! All is well and I am happy. If for a moment I am prevented or forget to pump energy into it, it shrinks, and then I am terrified; my lifeline is being cut! So whatever causes the manikin to shrink, to sink down or become less, whatever causes me real, acute pain, is like a little death. I will defend it and with my last ounce of energy, will try to keep it afloat up there. But such lavish expenditure of energy leaves little to spare for my ordinary, daily life activities. Hence I get easily tired and am under stress; I suffer from tension because I just cannot command enough energy for my ordinary tasks and chores.

These latter also bore me and I do not really want to attend to them because I have got such a demanding task to keep 'my' manikin floating up there. Hence the real difficulty inevitably encountered in any traditional training is to work up sufficient strength to starve the manikin of its energy input. This is far from easy; many little deaths need to be died for the manikin to come down. Only then is it possible to look at the place where one's feet stand and to find what is actually there.

Meanwhile we are divided, looking for something, searching for some kind of fulfilment, always with the idea that it is for me, that I need to be fulfilled, need to become whole — I this and I that. This is seeing it from the divided state, the feet going in one direction and the head looking in the other. To begin with, that is just as it is and cannot be helped. We must start from where we are, with what we have!

So when we set out on this journey, we must know what equipment we have available, and how to use it. It is no good to wish or wait for equipment like the Buddha's — we must start, and keep going. As Picture 1 portrays, in our divided state at first we are searching around for the 'right' way. I always want to be right — that is why I make so many mistakes. Once the initial inertia is overcome and we have started, many discoveries await us.

True, Daily Life Practice — just giving oneself to what now is being done anyway — sounds the simplest thing and not worth writing home about. It rather begs the question — and what then? But just try it, and go on doing so. It is the most difficult and vexatious thing possible; nothing simple or easy about it. There is one consolation, however: only a fully-fledged Buddha can do this practice perfectly! For us, the continuous training habituates us to it; and it also brings up new data, on the basis of which depends the next step. So 'I' cannot see or plan the next step; that is another lesson to be learnt. When we actually start this practice, giving ourselves into what at the moment we are doing is by no means so obvious or simple as we thought. It is also bound to bring up reactions, habits, attitudes, proclivities of which I was quite unaware. Just these are the data on which the next step depends.

How can I start cooking if I have never been in a kitchen and so do not know the most obvious things? Suppose one day I am looking through old junk and find my grandmother's recipe book and remember nostalgically that delicious cake she used to make. I find the recipe — goodness, how simple! Surely even I can follow that, though I have never bothered about cooking. So I buy all the ingredients as specified and now I am ready to start. I read again, 'Cream a knob of butter, add three spoonfuls of sugar and three egg yolks'. As I reach out to get that knob of butter, I find that I do not know what amount of butter that is. Never having been in a kitchen, I have never seen one. And coming now to think, three spoonfuls of sugar — flat or heaped? Teaspoons? Tablespoons? It says the proportions must be accurate! Nor do I know how to break an egg and separate the yolk from the white. But that need not yet bother me for I am still stuck with that knob of butter!

Training is also like that. It takes it for granted that some of the fundamentals are already familiar, not just in the head, but from practice with the body. If not available, we run into trouble or go grievously astray. Traditional meditation teachers do not talk about *Sila* practice; they take it for granted, or how could one otherwise think of taking up the discipline of meditation, a religious discipline which demands strength of perseverance against all the odds that are bound to arise? That strength accrues from *Sila* practice, without which attempts at meditation are bound to fail. To spell it out very clearly, the difference in strength is either I forcing myself to persevere to become somebody or get somewhere; or the strength that accrues from the Daily Life Practice, from whole-heartedly giving myself into what is now being done. The great example as well as inspiration for that is the Buddha under the Bo-tree; even Mara the tempter could not swerve him, daughters and demons alike failed.

When we read modern meditation manuals, the do-it-yourself type, they read like instructions for home improvement. Or like cooking recipes, they instruct, 'Place the mind here, now place it there, now lift it up from here and point it there,' and so on. It all sounds so easy until you try to do it. Just place your mind wherever you are told — on the tip of your nose, on a candle, on the abdomen, or nowhere at all — make it blank! And just stay like this for at least an hour or so. Try! Have you managed to place the mind thus and keep it there? Yes? For how long, uninterrupted? Of course I cannot — 'I the doer' cannot!

There is real work to be done. And no benefit accrues to me, for I am not even the doer, which is the first lesson I need to learn in this endeavour. In the beginning, of course, I cannot help but feel that I must do it. But if persisting long enough, I come to the conclusion that I cannot. And now with the ensuing frustration and disappointment, a counter-reaction sets in, 'For years I have been training, and no progress at all!' Which is true, for how can a delusion train or progress? So it is a question of just going on without any desire for profit or hankering after fame. I will not get anything out of it — I will not become better, I will not become famous, or a great practitioner, 'I' will not become a Buddha. The only thing I will become, all going well, is what I have always been — nothing. That is awakening from the delusion. I am afraid of that, because I cannot conceive the fullness of Not-I. So in a way I want to give myself into the practice, and in a way I am frightened of doing so, and hold back, get myself distracted or seek for evasions. Again, I am in a split state.

In Japan, with so many evergreen trees, it is said that the old leaves are kind, staying on and so protecting the new ones and falling off when the young buds are ready to sprout. Usually this is considered analogous to the relation of parent and child. But for Zen training, this may be taken in the way that somehow we have to start walking. We may not yet know where to, parted from ourselves as we are, but as long as we just keep going, willing to take things as they come and just open to the walking, a certain set of data accrues which is quite different from what I had always thought. If these data are taken in, 'incorporated', our old attitude begins to change and eventually falls off as now no longer effective or relevant. In its place a new one emerges, now more suitable to this stage of the training or development. So in the course of continuing training, ever new data emerge, bringing about further changes in attitude — a slow ripening or maturing in depth, little shift by little shift. All these soften up the rigid structure of I, and of fear born from the desire that I must be or get something, preferably something good, but anything rather than nothing.

Such little changes of attitude happen almost unnoticeably. Only by hindsight arises the awareness that what used to bother me now seems irrelevant and is no longer an issue. Notice that the 'me' is missing in this awareness; hence there is no bother! This is the secret of good training.

But there is also another side to these little shifts of attitude. We are great collectors! Having found a new attitude that has helped me at a specific stage and state, I now hold on to this as for dear life! Having once found it useful, I will not let it go. But however useful it might have been then, it is no longer so for the next step. This is one aspect of the Buddha's *Parable of the Raft*, not to trouble to carry it along once the other shore has been safely reached. So when we cling to this old leaf attitude, it cannot fall off though no longer appropriate. At that, the new attitude cannot emerge or if so, is warped or stunted. Again, what happens if we insist on moving forward the foot that has just taken a step? Yet one more step with the same foot, and now I am so split I can no longer move! In this plight I usually need to be told to stop trying and that now the other foot has to go forwards — which I had not thought of. Such analogies seem deceptively simple, but in fact are very helpful. Desire, wanting, is fundamental — one of the Three Fires, primal energy. It is therefore not a question of getting rid of it, but a question of the skilful use of the energy inherent in it rather than being swept away by it willy-nilly or refusing its energy altogether, which is unskilful. Basically, desire of any kind, for fame or gain, is connected with wanting 'more' (better, higher and so on). Which in itself already explains why we have so much trouble with letting anything go. Whatever I have acquired, by whatever means, has become my property, has it not? It belongs to me, is part of me. That is why losing it hurts! And here we have an indication of why some Zen stories recount drastic measures like hacking off an arm. It needs to be stressed that it is quite irrelevant whether such stories are historically true; we do not know; more likely they are not. True in the profoundest sense is what they portray, their message. Heeding that might prevent us from indulging in either extreme — arguing the historical 'fact' or literally imitating the 'act'.

Anyway, losing hurts. The less experience we have of it, the more trouble we have with it. Children, when playing games, used to learn to enjoy 'fair play' and 'good sport', and good luck to the winner. Nowadays it seems we cannot play any more; it is either a grim determination that, fair or foul, I must win; or 'competitive' sport or games are considered harmful. What nonsense — the whole nature, not only ours but of all that is, is built on and develops from the principle of what neutrally could be considered as 'utmost stretch'; otherwise we would all still be primal sludge.

So we have to relearn 'playing' and 'losing'. 'Let the heart not settle down on anything,' says the Diamond Sutra. This is a universal insight; nothing specifically Eastern about it. Surely we have all been brought up on Blake's, 'He who kisses the joy as it flies . . .'?

Where then is the trouble? If I have successfully brought off something, and now got myself into the habit of doing so, somehow this habit belongs to me, is the 'property' of me (not just mine) ; this is why I feel I cannot let it go, instead of always clearing, emptying, voiding, sweeping out. There is great merit in Sutra chanting. First, it fills the heart with aspiration for the Buddha's Path; being now filled with it, one might be tempted to keep it all for one's own use, for one's own walking on that Path. Actually we do not keep any of it but 'turn over' the merit, so that after having given ourselves into the chanting, we end it totally cleaned out, voided of anything. This cleanly becoming nothing at all, again and again — the daily chanting — makes it possible to come into accord with the Dharma, that is with our inherent nature. Having become estranged from it we are in a split state amid the tangle of the pairs of opposites, ensnared by the ten thousand things. If we are hesitant, unwilling to risk walking on from where our feet stand, thinking, 'No, I am not going to stir at all until I know exactly what I have to do, to say and to think; only then shall I start walking the Buddha's way, for then I'll be able to do it correctly,' we will sit for ever, preening ourselves with the delusion that if I but know how to do it I can do it. We learn by doing it, not by sitting and thinking how, for then we are stuck.

This sad state befell a centipede; capable of running very fast, it was asked, 'How can you keep all your feet under control, never get them crossed, never stumble? At such speed, too! And with which leg do you actually start to run?' The centipede began to think and found that he did not know. He went on thinking, trying to find out, but to no avail. He died on the spot, still busily thinking, 'How?' and incapable of moving!

So never mind how, just somehow start walking any old way, at least start moving. However halt or lame, even split from oneself, one learns from *doing* it. Being willing and eager to learn also makes one open to correction and this again helps in the little shifts of attitude and counteracts the clinging to 'my' way of doing which so often is different from the Buddha's Way! This is the gist of another Japanese proverb often heard in Zen training, 'Better than learning it, get used to it.' This also indicates that there is a strong physical aspect to the training; it is done more in the body than in the head.

So the herdsman, though split — that is, divided in himself — nevertheless starts walking. That is, aspiration and motivation have come together into one harmony. He has heard something of Buddhism, and understands that what he feels to be lacking is not to be found outside himself. But as yet this is only an intellectual understanding; underneath there is the feeling that something extra, additional, 'more' has to be found and 'incorporated' somehow.

II — FINDING THE TRACES

Reading the Sutras and listening to the teachings, the herdsman had an inkling of their message and meaning. He has discovered the traces. Now he knows that however varied and manifold, yet all things are of the one gold, and that his own nature does not differ from that of any other. But he cannot yet distinguish between what is genuine and what fake, still less between the true and the false. He can thus not enter the gate, and only provisionally can it be said that he has found the traces.

POEMS

1

Under the trees by the water, the bull's traces run here and there.

Has the herdsman found the way through the high,
    scented grass?

However far the bull now may run, even up the far mountains,

With a nose reaching up to the sky, he cannot hide himself
    any longer.

2

Many wrong paths cross where the dead tree stands by the rock.

Restlessly running round and round, in his little nest of grass,

Does he know his own error? In his search, just when his
    feet follow the traces,

He has passed the bull by and has let him escape.

3

Many have searched for the bull but few ever saw him.

Up north in the mountains or down in the south, did he
    find his bull?

The One Way of light and dark along which all come and go;

Should the herdsman find himself on that Way he need not
    look further.

Picture 2

FINDING THE TRACES

Here a certain amount of new data has been collected already. In our case, the herdsman has found the Buddha's teachings and 'discovered' some of his own ingrained habits and attitudes. He knows roughly in which direction he is to go. He has heard of deliverance, and wants to go towards it. So his feet and his head have come together. He now knows what he is after, his own heart-bull; but this is still only intellectual knowledge. Actually the bull has never been missing. But the man 'has lost sight' — has become unconscious — of his bull, and so thinks he must look for him outside.

Because we make concrete pictures of what 'I want' and chase after them, we make mistake after mistake. Still, and in spite of all the mistakes, a real compulsion — inborn urge — forces the lifelong quest after the own heart. It is pitiful, ludicrous really, and yet so wonderful and mysterious, this our desperate looking for something that has never gone missing!

In this the heart itself connives. In its desire to be re-discovered, it stages self-portraits! From time to time it seems to jump out from our chest and make itself perceptible by draping itself like a shimmering, fascinating veil over something which now beckons from outside and is of irresistible allure. After all, one cannot exist without a heart, and if one's very heart is thus perceived as outside, one cannot help but go after it — with which we are in the region of the Fires, of the afflicting passions, in short, of delusion.

I once heard a Thai teacher describe such delusory afflictions. Chuckling, he told us, 'There are silly monks, too, and I shall tell you of one of them, ha, ha! He was sitting in his little meditation hut in the dark of night, when suddenly he saw jumping before him a beautiful golden ball that rolled away into the jungle. It was so beautiful, and he ran after it. The ball kept rolling, and whenever the monk nearly caught up with it and tried to catch it, it rolled away a little faster. He kept after it as it rolled here and there all through the jungle on ever more entangled paths. Once he nearly caught it, but it jumped out of reach up a tree, that beautiful golden ball. He climbed after it, for he knew he had to have it — life was not worth living without; it was too beautiful, enthralling! So he had to go after it, shinning up that tree. The golden ball got higher and higher and then started to roll along a big branch with the monk still in hot pursuit. The branch started to sway perilously under the weight of the monk, and at that, the golden ball vanished. 'Coming to himself' again, the monk found himself high up in a tree on a very exposed branch and was terrified. He could not climb down; in fact, he dared not move, and yelled for help. He had to call for hours until the other monks heard and helped him down. What had happened? Ha, ha! — one does not let one's heart run away from one!'

Usually it takes a very dangerous moment or utter exhaustion for the heart to jump back again; this is why the monk on his perilous branch lost sight of the golden ball. And when he 'woke up', was frightened at seeing where he was! It is the same with us, too. And such bewitchment or its opposite can last a very long time. That monk was lucky.

How often does our heart jump out and we pursue the

shimmering object that keeps rolling from us or before us? Profit, fame, a new hat, the best sports car, a house, the beloved, Enlightenment, Satori — or whatever!

How can we find that heart, for it is not always in the form of a golden ball, is it? Sometimes it is very different from one. So what is this heart? Bodhidharma's famous stanza states,

> 'A special transmission outside the teachings.
> Not depending on written words.
> Directly pointing to the human heart,
> Seeing into its nature and becoming Buddha.'

Seeing into the nature of the human heart is becoming at one with it, with its inherent energy which, remembering that golden ball, is tremendous. Since we somehow belong together, it forces us to go after it; we cannot help but do so. While deluded by its play of forms — the golden ball — it misleads, like a will-o'-the-wisp.

So we can take it that the human heart — obviously by this we do not mean the physical organ — is actually nothing but tremendous energy. But not the human heart only; this energy (we call it 'energy' for want of a better word) is the original nature or true nature of all that is. It functions as is appropriate to the form — in a mouse as a mouse, in a hungry ghost as a hungry ghost. In spring the first blades of crocus seemingly pierce through the still half-frozen ground — yet when touched they feel as soft as fine hair; what gives them the strength? When their season comes, they move and push, obeying their own nature, which is also Nature with which they are in accord. In their season, the petals unfold — that is the way they are: their nature and Nature are one. Even if blighted, they still fulfill themselves, obeying their nature and Nature — for the two are not two but one. In the human realm this is little understood and often badly misinterpreted or misused because we are not inhabitants of the human realm but vagrants through all six states of being. Actually, it is just this misunderstanding which is the delusion that seemingly binds us onto the Wheel of Becoming, of Change.

But back to the crocuses — the strength to push through the hard ground is not 'theirs' but is the whole force, strength, energy, or power of Nature with which they are in harmony, and which functions also in their nature. So they are in accord with Nature, with what is, the seasons and conditions. Crocuses are not desert flowers. Unlike us, they are not blindly impulsive, self-biased. We are again reminded that 'the passions are the Buddha-Nature and the Buddha-Nature is the passions'. The sense of I, which warps the energy into the afflicting passions, is also the basic delusion which works our suffering by binding us onto the Wheel of Becoming or Change; while thus I-biased, we are less than human!

As an ideal to strive towards, a Chinese Classic, the *Tao Te Ching* (The Way and its Virtue/Power) describes this harmony, by virtue of which the strength or power of Nature can function freely in the individual form. 'Man obeys the laws of earth. Earth obeys the laws of Heaven. Heaven obeys the laws of Tao. Tao obeys the laws of its own Nature.' In the case of sentient beings like us, harmony with nature is harmony with the human heart (not mine), and this is what Bodhidharma stresses, 'Directly pointing to the human heart, seeing into its nature, and becoming Buddha.' This seeing is to be understood as once again becoming one with that nature, and thus once more being in harmony with it and hence also with the strength or power that is its function. Nothing can be said of the Nature itself; it is perceptible only in its function. It is not, repeat not, an I seeing into any nature, either mine or other; all this is merely intellectual entertainment which cannot bring deliverance or insight.

Harmony with nature is harmony with all that is, hence with the way all things really are as well as with the human heart. This profound relationship is what the insight of the Buddha entails, is the Dharma. To come into harmony with this nature, with this Dharma, and with the way it works, is what the heart yearns for. Insight into it also re-links again with the full power of the human heart that is at one with Nature. It is only my lopsided, partial seeing, my making 'graven images' such as a golden ball, that sends me running after gain and fame, blinding and entangling me again and again.

So in Picture 2 the man is now truly on his way. But though we may have heard of heart and harmony, and also of the deceptive golden ball, more often than not we first come into contact with the full energy of the human heart as something quite different. We are inevitably entirely unprepared for such an encounter with this power — consciously, that is, for actually we are not unfamiliar with it!

What happens truly when, rushing round a corner, we run into each other and inadvertently you tread on my toe? When the pain sears through the body, who will feel, 'Well it just hurts,' with truly no other feeling than just the pain, and try to deal with that? That may be on the sixth remove; but if aware and honest, what is the first reaction to that sudden encounter and searing pain, the natural reaction? Even if able to restrain the hand and tongue (which means remaining outwardly at least human and not becoming a fighting demon all out), something snorts up at that moment, does it not, at the impact and pain? And what thus snorts up is not tame, nor is it something paltry. There is a strength and wildness in it that is certainly not human. We must never forget that. But splendid it is, and intensely alive; it is also highly dangerous.

To learn to deal with this as the first manifestation of the bull, as its traces, is extremely difficult, because when it snorts up with such power, I am no longer there! Thus I never can witness it. This is the difficulty at Picture 2. The man looks for a golden ball and does not realise what the wild (black) heart-bull actually looks like. Rather, he looks for something great, for beauty, for the Buddha's virtue, power and insight — not for the snorting eruptions that occur umpteen times a day! So, to begin with, he cannot even find the traces. Nor does he want to see them, for 'I am not like that!' 'Well, I know I am not perfect,' say I modestly but deep inside me is nevertheless a conviction that I am the hub and centre of the universe, though modesty forbids me from saying so. I mean, I am not exactly a wild animal, am I? I am fairly reasonable, quite decent really, and have no quarrel with you — but why did you tread on my toe? I would not have suffered such an uproar if you had been just a bit more careful. Look what you have done to me! Hurt me, even made me lose my temper! You may not have done it intentionally, but clearly it is your fault that this has happened to me, not mine!

Now just stop and look. Have I ever had such a snorting uproar? I am inclined to deny it — with good conscience perhaps, because at the moment I have forgotten that such uproars occur often enough. And because I feel that I ought not to have them, I do not want to take responsibility for them and so I blame you as 'my' scapegoat. And because of this 'hiding', the energy has always remained primitive, wild, not 'brought up'.

A Zen poem precisely describes this situation. We may think of a man who has trained a little, has heard of the Buddha's Way of deliverance, wants to walk it, and so is having no truck with those snorters. He is now determined to meditate, the hopeful escape away from all snorters. But — and this is now the poem — 'On a lotus leaf sits a frog, legs crossed, hands folded, back straight, motionless, deep in meditation. Behind him rears up a huge snake. Does he know? Does he not know? On the lotus leaf sits a frog, legs crossed, hands folded, back straight, motionless, deep in meditation — WATCH OUT!'

Do we watch out? Do we turn round and recognize the snake as ourselves? Have we the strength, the courage to say,

'Yes, that is also me,' and to do something with it? Instead of being once more gobbled up by the snake? That serpent has truly been with us since the days we lost paradise. The snake mythology is a fascinating one; itself 'unseen' — 'Get thee behind me, Satan' — and 'There are none so blind as those who do not wish to see' — it just keeps on gobbling up the frog. Thus the seeming bondage of the Wheel, bondage by the afflicting passions. But there is also the wisdom of the serpent, and of the snake that is portrayed as a circle, with its tail in its own mouth, devouring itself as well as ever continuing. What better symbol do we need to point at the possibility of transformation of the serpent power into the 'Wisdom Gone Beyond'?

The Buddha found the Way out of afflictions and suffering. In the above analogy this begins when the frog takes heed and looks at the snake, and the snake looks at the frog, and they suddenly recognize each other. Then they begin to have respect as well as tolerance for each other. But though their families are fairly close, both have to change a good deal until they finally can merge into one.

So the man looking for the traces finally stumbles upon them — not in the sublime scriptures where he thought they were, far above everything that bothers him. The traces are right in the middle of daily life, amid our daily chores, troubles and hang-ups, and they are conspicuous. Once they have been found and acknowledged as the traces of the bull, wherever I look, there are traces everywhere. That produces the first serious upset in the practice.

'What have I let myself in for? I am getting worse instead of better! This is not leading out of suffering.' But factually this only goes to show that the practice works. For it is not that I am getting worse, it is only that I am beginning to see what actually is there, and always has been there. Little by little the defence screens behind which I habitually hide myself are beginning to give way and dissolve; and with that a first awareness arises of what formidable task is ahead.

Much energy is needed for that task. And there is also the need to examine those traces most carefully. First of all, beware of golden balls, for these are the most dangerous and treacherous! It is much better just to look for the ordinary traces of losing one's temper; of greediness; of refusal and resentment; of passionate, stubborn, opinionated flare-ups, however small or 'justified'. So again, rather than being deceived by a golden ball, the ordinary traces of 'don't want', 'don't like', 'won't', 'must have' are good enough to start with. They are also of an energy potential that can just about be endured, without being carried away at least to some extent. It is a twenty-four hour occupation to be open to the impact of such traces; that is 'looking for the traces' honestly, not denying them or blaming somebody else, wanting to seem better than I actually am. For the traces of the bull do not signify an enemy that should be got rid of, but rather precious energy of sufficient power to grind, burn or singe away 'I'. This powerful energy, being much stronger than I, needs to be approached religiously, respectfully, with folded hands, 'The Fires still burn, I am still here, please burn me away.' That is what purification really means in the religious life, and why bowing is so important. Only the precious energy that flares up in the Fires has the strength actually to change I, and itself also changes in that process. So follow those traces gratefully but carefully, and gently — that is the purpose of the exercise.

When we started searching for the bull, we had 'ideas', that is, mental pictures about him which prevented recognition. Or it could also be said that the bull was hiding behind these pictures, or that he was hidden behind them — both apply.

When we suddenly stumble across him, it is uncommonly difficult to recognize the heart-bull, though actually he has never been absent. Even if searching for him, we tend to look in just one direction and so usually miss him; and when he is actually there in front of us, we refuse to see him because we are blinded by the veils of our delusion.

Thus finding the traces is not easy. Moreover, it takes great courage actually to recognize the traces, to affirm and verify them as such, and say, 'Yes, that is of the heart-bull, is me.' But this means abstaining from our usual scapegoat evasions of blaming something or somebody else — you, the circumstances, the establishment, or whatever, anything rather than my cherished opinions!

I had been in Japan five years when a friend at home, who was having a very difficult time, wrote to me, 'You in your cloistered peace! What do you know of the problems that beset us in the world?' He knew that as a woman I went to the monastery for training or work, but did not sleep there. So in my replies I pointed out to him that the cloister is not of itself peaceful, nor is the world troublesome. There is not all that much difference between outside and inside. Whether I am angry or upset because the head monk scolds me, perhaps even for something that I have not done, or whether upset about something in the office, or at school, being upset is the same. If the monks leave me the worst places to weed or sweep leaves, especially in winter when half under snow, or whether my colleagues in the office leave me more than my fair share of work, the grating against it is in me! What produces it is really irrelevant. As long as there is grating in me, any situation will produce it, and if there is no 'legitimate' outlet, it will produce its own release, i.e. fasten on anything! So not the cloister, but work with that grating is important.

A cloister is not a haven of peace, nor is it an escape. If we live in the world, we have a job, a home, perhaps a family. So I can escape, for if there is grating against my work, I can leave it behind and go home. Even though I may carry a certain amount with me, mostly I can leave behind what aggravates me. If I have trouble at home, I can escape from it to my place of work. But in a monastery, there is no such escape. One is continuously in that surrounding that chafes and grates. At home, too, or at work, someone may almost take on the features of a demon, or persecutor, but then we can escape. In a monastery we cannot, and so really it is very much a grinding situation, grinding off excrescences! That cloistered peace takes a very long time to be established; they say about seven to nine years minimum. Until then, it needs to be endured. This endurance is a very formative process.

As we begin to find the traces in our gratings and gripings, we actually become familiar with ourselves, with how we habitually react. We suffer from great deception about ourselves; though we truly believe we know ourselves, yet we really do not.

In my own experience, I used to believe that I could not live without music. Even in Japan I soon acquired a little radio. A day during which I could not hear any music was somehow incomplete. Yet I found that if occasionally a friend invited me to go to a concert, though with shining eyes I would say, 'Yes, I would love to,' when the time approached, particularly in winter, and if it meant going by slow tram to an unheated concert hall and coming back late and very cold, yet having to get up early next morning to go to the monastery — well, I looked for excuses to cry off! The third time this happened I began to wonder whether it was really fair to accept only to cancel at the last moment. From that I began to realise that although I loved music, I did not love it as much as I thought; other considerations could override it. On the other hand, I also became aware that summer or winter, snow or rain or shine, I managed somehow to have a walk, even an occasional good long tramp. Somehow I always seemed to find the time, or time miraculously happened to become available! So from what I actually did and not from what I thought, I learnt what my real preferences were! I still consider it one of my greatest discoveries, finding out that what I actually did was different from what I thought my preferences were.

Along such lines we can find the traces of the bull. But since the Middle Way is remarkably difficult to keep to, one can now veer off into the other extreme, and become dazzled and attached to the new-won insight! Hence, having just learnt how important my walk was to me, I may begin to feel that if I cannot have that walk then I cannot endure the long evening sitting! So back to the Middle Way, where both extremes, 'must have' and 'can't do without' (both sharing the common denominator I), undergo transformation by 'walking on'. It requires long and patient training.

Thus we find the traces of the bull and discover the beginning of the Middle Way — the Buddha's Way. It is helpful to bear in mind that the first teaching the Buddha gave to his erstwhile disciples, the five monks who by their long practice were qualified or ready to hear it, was that of the Middle Way! Only then did he present the Four Noble Truths.

'The Great Way is not difficult; it only avoids picking and choosing.' But picking and choosing, and thus preferences, are natural in any sentient being. The very way we move or walk is individually different; friends can recognise each other by the way they walk, even if seen from far off. Is that picking and choosing? Should I now train myself to walk in a 'universal' way? Is that 'universal' way so uniform that there is no distinction? It is still all picking and choosing, is it not? All 'I', the doer!

There is still another type of preference, very different from the natural one. It can be clearly distinguished by its energy content which is so powerful that I feel 'I must have' or 'can't do without' whatever it is. How do we in daily life become aware of that type? Well, as for me, I usually drink coffee, but in the afternoon I prefer tea. And if a friend who knows me well gives me a cup of tea in the morning, that is one of the tests. Do I say thanks for the tea and drink it, or do I feel aggrieved, even angry, react against it? 'She knows I like coffee!' Complaint, irritation, annoyance, instead of gratitude for the cup of tea! That is when my choosing makes the energy erupt as Fire, invades the natural preference, and 'heats' it.

There is nothing wrong with the natural preferences as such; as long as there is a body, there will be preferences. And if I cannot have 'my' want (or wish) now, that is all right, too. But if the preferences become inflated to 'I must have or I cannot go on', then, metaphorically, we are in bull country and clearly can see his traces. As we get familiar with them, we learn also to read them; how he was stumping and rampaging around but was too quick to be seen. He is already away — only the traces remain.

As familiarity increases and we get closer to the heated ambience of the bull, some important discoveries await us! So, whenever we come across those fancies of the mind that seem — to me — the most lucid logic, basic assumptions that all know, laws on which the world is built on, that is where we have to watch out. They are likely to be mine only and by no means shared by everybody else. Though I may think coffee the best drink except in the afternoon, that does not mean that you have — even less ought to have — the same liking for coffee. To realise at least some of the ramifications of this is having found the traces.

III — FINDING THE BULL

The herdsman recoils startled at hearing the voice and that instant sees into the origin. The six senses are quieted in peaceful harmony with the origin. Revealed, the bull in his entirety now pervades all activities of the herdsman, present as inseparably as is salt in sea water, or glue in paint. When the herdsman opens his eyes wide and looks, he sees nothing but himself.

POEMS

1

Suddenly a bush warbler trills high in the tree top.

The sun shines warm, and in the light breeze the willows
on the water's edge show their new green.

There is no longer a place where the bull can hide himself;

No painter can capture that magnificent head with its soaring
horns!

2

On seeing the bull and hearing his bellow,

Tai-sung, the painter, surpassed his craft.

Accurately he pictured the heart-bull from head to tail,

And yet, on carefully looking, he is not quite complete.

3

Having pushed his face right against the bull's nose,

He no longer needs to follow the bellowing.
This bull is neither white nor blue.

Quietly nodding, the herdsman smiles to himself.

Such landscape cannot be caught in a picture!

Picture 3

SEEING THE BULL

How now to go on with the practice? Recognising the traces and following them in our search for that elusive heart-bull is the next step.

In the actual situation, my friend has just handed me that cup of tea and something snorts up in me! If really careful in the training, at this moment there is instant awareness of what is happening: the bull snorting! So far I had always denied him; now for the first time I actually 'see' him. Hence I can no longer blame my friend but realise it is me, and finally after long training I have eventually come into contact with the heart-bull. There is a hot moment when that awareness hits me. Then I want to grasp, hold, to look and see what the bull is like; and what happens? All I see is that the bull has already gone. Only fleetingly I saw his hind quarter, and the whisk of his tail!

These pictures are remarkably accurate. The moment I want to hold, to look, to inspect — he is gone. This is rather frustrating. It also indicates how split I am from myself. My usual way of looking at something is so as to recognise it or to learn it, not a coming together with it. I can look at the lines on my hand, and I can give a lucid description of them only because there is a distance. We are split, my hand and I! If my hand hits my cheek, at the moment of impact — at-one-ment — is there anything that I can say about the lines on my hand? But the impact is there. That is the difference between knowing by observation, 'in the head', and knowing by familiarity, 'in the body', for which no observation is necessary; as with the impact, it just happens, or better, IS. Such awareness arises of itself, direct and immediate; Zen Buddhism, all Buddhism, is referring to this type.

The immediacy of such incoming information is easily demonstrable. Just pinch yourself in the soft part of the arm; does the awareness of the pinch arise of itself, force itself into consciousness, not needing an act of observation? As that it is the direct perception of the pinch, rather than a descriptive commentary. As when drinking a glass of water, one 'instantly' knows how cold it is.

Having found the traces, we understand that things are all of the same dough, however differently they may be formed. All things are Buddha things. We are all sitting in the same boat. We all have the same reactions, although they are triggered off by different things connected with the preferences of the body and the inner framework that we partly are born with, and which partly we have made since then. Yet the Buddha-Nature is in all of us; our reaction mechanism is the same; we all have our share of the heart-bull.

At stage two we cannot distinguish between what is genuine and what is not, even less between true and false. There are only the traces as yet, accurate as that, but also deceptive because they are not the bull! To distinguish between the true and false without judging is not yet possible. 'Direct perception' has not yet taken place; only the traces have been found.

But following those traces and coming closer, at hearing the bellow, the herdsman suddenly is startled out of himself, and jolted into the origin — he catches sight of the bull. That means that he did enough training not to be deceived, has now enough inner strength to stay at home, can endure and witness the impact — or an eruption of the fires flaring up — without being carried away on the wave of that energy.

Now we can come back yet again to the friend with the cup of tea. Being convinced that it was all the friend's fault — thus evading the issue — is now no longer possible. Factually, at being handed the cup of tea, there was a hot eruption coming up. It is this hot reaction in the actual situation that we have to work with, aware that it is my own heart rolling helter-skelter like that golden ball we talked about, and refraining from running after it and going astray. In fact, the bull in his entirety has for a moment been glimpsed, the voice has been heard. Now truly known by that impact-awareness, he cannot hide himself any longer. Hence the realisation that he, the bull, is inherently present as salt in sea water.

Master Hakuin has a most helpful analogy about sea water. If a man really wants to know the taste of sea water, rather than speculating about it, all he need do (Japan is an island) is just go out of his front door and continue going in a straight line. Sooner or later he will arrive at the sea shore. There, stooping down, he puts his hand into the sea, and licks off a few drops; at that instant he knows the taste of all the seven oceans!

The passions are the Buddha-Nature and the Buddha-Nature is the passions. Care needs to be taken with such stark and startling statements. So before I let rip in all directions at once, thus showing my Buddha-Nature, I had better restrain myself and ponder for a while. Could it be the same tremendous energy or power that, albeit blind, acts in the passions? And that this same energy, but transformed — humanised, spiritualised — is the Buddha-Nature? In the presence of I with my picking and choosing, this energy flares up as the bull, but in the absence of I — No-I as the Buddha put it — it reverts to what it always has been, the Buddha-Nature. Awareness of that energy, at the moment of eruption, is catching the bull.

IV — CATCHING THE BULL

For the first time today he encountered the bull that for so long had been hiding in the wilderness. But his pleasantly familiar wilderness still attracts the bull strongly. He yearns for the sweet-smelling grass and is difficult to hold. Stubborn self-will rages in him and wild animal-nature rules him. If the herdsman wants to make the bull really gentle, he must discipline him with the whip.

POEMS

1

With great effort the herdsman succeeded in catching the bull.
But stubborn, wilful and strong, this bull is not easily gentled!
At times he breaks out and climbs up to the high plains,
Or rushes down into foggy marshlands to hide himself there.

2

Hold the rein tight and do not let go.
Many of the subtlest faults are not yet up-rooted.
No matter how gently the herdsman pulls at the nose-rope,
The bull may still rear and try to bolt back to the wild.

3

Though caught where the sweet-scented grass reaches sky-high,
The herdsman must not let go of the rein tied to the bull's nose.
Though the way home beckons clearly already,
The herdsman must often halt with the bull, by the blue
       stream or on the green mountain.

Picture 4

CATCHING THE BULL

How is the bull caught? So far he used to evade being caught — he reared and ran, and only the hind-quarters could be seen. Factually, his power is so great that he bowls me over — so I feel that he is too quick; by the time I remember to catch him, he is already gone! But this is because as yet I do not really know the heart-bull. I have really only seen his hind-quarters and wagging tail! When we have truly become familiar with our actions and reactions, as distinct from what we think them to be, we become capable of 'staying at home' when the bull snorts up. We no longer try to grasp and look and deliberate, but rather as daily life practice has enabled us to do, we open up and say, 'Yes'.

At that moment we have the bull. He, of course, wants to rush off as always. What usually happened was that the bull snorted up, and I either turned my back on him, somewhat shakily pretending he was not there at all because, already gone, I could not see him! Or, more likely, in his sudden and snorting emergence, he has taken me on his back and carried me away with him to wherever it is: the green lush valleys of sensual pleasure, or the high plains of intellectual gymnastics, even the peaks of high fancies! If at the moment of the bull rising there is both recognition and acceptance, then he cannot take me on his back, and is himself caught. The well-known danger of being carried away by an onslaught of the passions is echoed in a Chinese proverb, 'He who bestrides the tiger may not dismount.' Tiger or bull, once he has got me on his back, there is not much that I can do, bar holding on and hoping that neither of us will come to much harm.

A good example is riding. Once we let the horse break away, having panicked or whatever, no matter how soft its mouth is, it is not in a state to feel the reins any more and all one can do is hold on and hope for the best until it has tired itself out and comes to itself again, all passions spent.

It does sound familiar? The cure for such dangerous bolting in horse or bull is to turn round and at the same speed go back to where we started from! Can we remember — wherever we have strayed to and 'find' ourselves, to go at once right back to what is being done! While being carried away, nothing much can be done. We are no longer capable of perceiving anything, our seeing and perception are wholly beclouded by the 'Fires'; we see and perceive with the bull's eyes! So for that time and in that state, we are the bull!

We have to be careful. Thus fired and carried away, a really creative act may happen, for the bull is both above and below the human realm. It is also true that the greatest and most fiendish atrocities occur in the state of being carried away by the bull. So it is most important that we get to know what he actually is; also get to know that while being fired or possessed or carried away by him, we are no longer human. We have been returned to the elemental state of nature, of sheer creation and destruction. Not beyond good and bad, but below good and bad; not yet human. This is a very dangerous state and so we have every reason to get to know the bull, to catch him and be willing to work with him, really to gentle him. Our own heart-nature is the bull, and it can be very dangerous to ourselves and to others if he is roaming wild. It begs to be gentled. Bull and man need each other, need to be re-united once more and thus made whole again!

What is the wilderness in which the bull roams? 'Oh, I wish things could be different! Then the world would be a better place!' 'I can't go on any more today — it is just too tiring. Just a little rest. Now it is just not possible any more.' Or I must take issue with something, or tell somebody off 'for his own good'. That wilderness is truly illimitable! Looking at the outside only, the circumstances, the situation, but never looking inside; how difficult it is to recognise the bull, and then to acknowledge him. We 'want' to see him — but only as a picture! We squirm and devise a hundred subterfuges to avoid seeing the bull as he is. Hence the enormous effort needed — for there are none so blind as those who do not wish to see! Moreover, the bull is the last thing I want to work with. I would rather take the whole world on my shoulders and make it a better place, more like what I want it to be, than just change the one thing that is possible for me to change — myself.

So the training, the work of gentling, is far from easy. Worse, the bull is not only wild, he is also extremely deceptive. Sometimes he snorts up wild and crude; but in normal circumstances, and when we are not under too much stress, we have more or less learnt how to behave in a human way. However angry I may be, I try to behave in a reasonable way. If my friend hands me that cup of tea, being under Buddhist training, I manage to say, 'Thank you,' but inside it is 'Blast you!' That is all right to begin with: at least I have said thank you. Good manners are the first discipline. We learn step by step. But the bull whispers, 'Perhaps I ought not to have said this; I should have been honest and said, Blast you! because that is what I felt.' Bah! Are we on the Buddha's Path or among the fighting demons? Even animals have their regulated 'manners'!

The bull is both subtle and wily. Once the obvious, crude and coarse outbursts have been gentled, he changes his tactics. 'I have done my best, and now I really must lie down and rest.' Since it is the heart-bull, one cannot help but feel compassion for that poor exhausted bull and is inclined to let him have a breather! But if you look very carefully at the poor beastie, you see that he has one eye cocked alertly, waiting his chance! Yes, a wily creature, and so the wiliness is in us too. We truly need to be familiar with ourselves as well as not taking ourselves too seriously. We need that kind of humour which is almost sportive play, in which neither of us really wins, but equally, neither really loses.

As children we wrestle with each other just for the fun of it, and although each tries to win, it does not matter all that much. What matters is that in so doing we become familiar with each other, with the ways and the strength of each other. That is what working with the bull actually entails, once he is caught.

So, having caught the bull, working together with him, and gentling him, begins. The bull is accustomed to his wilderness in which he has been allowed to roam for so long. We thought we knew ourselves, and had no idea that something like the bull actually existed. After that first shock of hearing his bellow and of meeting him, all black, he can no longer evade us; and as we get less frightened of his bellowing, we no longer turn away. So we have met, come together, crashed into each other, and at that moment recognised each other inherently as one.

Again, the picture shows this well: the rope holds or binds the two together, and it holds however they might strain apart, each wanting to have his own way. Now, known to each other, they can no longer break apart. True, the bull, still wild and used to his wilderness, may yet manage to run off and drag the herdsman with him, but when he gets tired, the herdsman drags him back again.

This working with him is the process of making the bull gentle. He cannot yet detach himself from the desire for the sweet grass. Look at the picture: he is a splendid bull, no doubt;

his soaring horns, all that strength that I lack — strength of endurance, strength of sticking it out — it is the bull's.

Home beckons already, for if the bull is truly gentled, that is the end of loneliness, the end also of feeling a gaping hole somewhere in my midriff, something missing in my life. This is precisely from where the bull has gone missing; and reunited, that aching void, which made me restlessly look for something to fulfil me, is filled.

Therefore we need to come together with the bull in spite of the fact that stubborn self-will rages in him, and wild animal nature rules him. But we need to take care, need careful training. Who would easily admit of him- or herself that stubborn self-will rages in me and wild animal nature rules me? I shy away from such insights, try to cover them up, and reassure myself once more. Surely this is not true; after all, I am a human being, reasonably behaved — as long as everything goes well. Yes, but then, what happens if my will is radically crossed, one of my ingrained notions is contested? If I am honest, what then happens? Do I mind? Do I then meekly say, 'Well, if you say so'? Or is it a case of stubborn self-will raging, and wild animal nature snorting? It is hard to be that honest because we do so want to be right, don't we? There is a lot of training to be done, not only with the bull, but with our willingness to give house-room to the bull. To say yes and make room for him when he snorts up; the body is geared to take the shock and contain the energy — 'I' cannot! That is another lesson to be learned.

What really happens when something we do not fancy comes flying at us? A snort — that is first! After that, depending on how we are individually geared, we react in one of two ways. Both are within us, but one is usually more dominant. I either hit out at what comes at me, a forward motion, aggression; or I shrink back into myself, cuddling myself defensively, 'least in sight', a backward motion. Either the hitting or the retreating attitude is how I usually face the situation, but not exclusively;

the other attitude may take over in certain circumstances. Both happen to go into gear of themselves, even against my will, and often to my surprise as when I set out on a certain course of action and find myself after a blind spot acting differently from, if not contrary to, what I had planned.

As to the other immediate gesture which displays the dominant attitude, shrinking back indicates retreat, not only from the outside threat but also from the energy snorting up within, warding it off. The energy gets thus repressed, pushed back and may then smoulder, turn sour or vindictive. If the display is of the active, want to hit out type, the energy is discharged in the act, or into the surroundings. There is also a kind of half-hearted, intentional way of really wanting to hit but not daring to, and so holding in, squeezing the energy which then, like in a hose pipe, hisses up, forming long thought-streams of what I should have done and said, which replays itself in the head again and again until the 'heat' that had arisen has exhausted itself again!

This energy arises in the body and so it is in the body that it has to be worked with. Zen training is not mental training or mind training, nor mental gymnastics, but a religious discipline to be undergone, reverently! The stress is on reverently and religious. For only then, instead of the bull running off again — a flash of hind-quarters and a wag of his tail — we actually crash into each other and connect again, as symbolised by the rope. 'Catching the Bull' is to say 'yes' at the moment of impact, and with a deep in-breath give house-room to this tremendous energy that has soared up — letting it fill me, enduring the charge. Refused or deluded, it is and acts as the bull; but in moments of danger, it is suddenly with us, helper, friend and guardian that takes over. So, making the body as large as possible — hence the in-breath — and saying yes to it, is giving it house-room. To endure the presence without being carried away or deflected then becomes the religious way, the enduring way, the reverent way. Bowing in front of that tremendous energy, 'The Fire still burns; I am still here, please burn me away!' and allowing the fire to do the burning is going through the Fire of purification, again and again!

What does burning in the fire feel like? If it is 'Yes, dear fire, go on burning me,' I am only fooling myself. There is no fire burning at all, because if there is real fire, there is real conflict, and then I have to clench my teeth and endure patiently and willingly, live through what seems unendurable! A conflict rages, perceptible by the clamping of the shoulders and general tensing up — hands, arms, stomach. The important thing now is not to be blinded and swept away by the picture-maker, not to judge and name as 'want' or 'anger', to think of nothing but precious energy arising. 'Yes, precious energy, please burn me away.'

Does that give an intimation why the Third Patriarch said that the Great Way is not difficult, it only avoids picking and choosing? Or why the Fourth Patriarch suggested sticking to the root and not bothering about the branches?

If I seek a culprit, a scapegoat, 'explanations' like the man shot with the poisoned arrow, all that precious energy is dissipated. What a waste! And what murky turbulence this results in. Better gratefully make use of the precious energy that has arisen, for I cannot summon it up by an act of will. Moreover, it is the only power in the universe great enough to have any inroad on me , on the deep root of stubborn self-will and wild animal nature! This is the energy of the bull; and by patient training, by enduring the conflict, the energy itself becomes transformed, gentled — less bull, more human.

So the work is between I and the bull; seemingly being two different entities, but at bottom the same, only having become estranged from each other. Remember, we seemed two opposite forces, each in the beginning not even aware of the other, refusing to see the other, not wanting the other. While one is up, the other is hidden. In cold blood, not fired, we are reasonable, decent chaps; we cannot even imagine what we can say or do when in a temper. When cooled down again from such a fired state, I can only say, 'I do not know what came over me; I must have been beside myself.' The two estranged sides are mutually exclusive; it is not easy for me to become aware of the other. This is what makes finding the traces and catching sight of the bull so difficult. It is very hard to say yes to him, to allow his presence without being carried away by him, and yet not refusing or repressing him either. I may know my peccadillos and attempt to rid myself of them, but ineffectively, because to do so I must learn to endure them without either giving in or trying to shove them away. As I am unaware of my real volcanic eruption zones, familiarity with the bull is sure to acquaint me with them.

If we can bear the presence of the bull without giving way to him, in this grappling with the bull we become aware that he is truly our own nature and much stronger than I. For the first time we also become aware that we are working with something from which we have never been parted. This is a very decisive stage. If we do not now open the eyes and take a good look, we slither headlong into a new mistake. Hence to make the bull really gentle, he must be disciplined with the whip. If we cannot work that discipline with our own heart-bull, he will remain wild. His stubborn self-will and his animal nature will continue to rule, not only the bull, but us too. Perhaps we can gloss it over, become hypocritical, but underneath it is still there.

A verse from the Dhammapada, a popular scripture of the Southern School says:

> To avoid doing evil,
> To do good,
> To purify the heart;
> That is the teaching of all the Buddhas.

Truly and always to avoid one and do the other is possible only for the fully purified heart, and so they go hand in hand; but the stress is on the avoiding evil and doing good, as much as possible, for this is the purification and is also the gentling of our own heart-bull. An early Chinese Zen master said to a great Confucian scholar who objected to the simplicity of the above verse, 'Though a little child may know this verse by heart, yet even a man of eighty fails to live up to it!'

Perhaps we can now see where the real gentling of the Bull takes place. It is our own stubborn self-will and wild animal nature that need the gentling, and therefore need the whip. We ourselves must have the determination to apply it — nobody can do it for us. We also need skill in this application, for, 'If the cart sticks in the mire, do you whip the cart or the ox?' At this crucial stage, not for a moment can we allow ourselves to drop the rein, or, as Daito Kokushi from his death-bed admonished his disciples, 'Strive diligently, strive diligently!' Truly, all who have gone the Buddha's Way speak with the same voice.

V — GENTLING THE BULL

If but one thought arises, then another and another follows in an endless round. Through awakening, everything becomes truth; through delusion, it becomes error. Things do not come into being depending on circumstances but arise from the herdsman's own heart. Hold the rein tight and do not allow any wavering.

POEMS

1

Not for a moment may the herdsman drop whip and rein,

Or the bull would break free and stampede into the dust.

But once patiently trained and made truly gentle,

He follows the herdsman without halter or chain.

2

Now the bull may saunter through the hill forests,

Or else walk the much travelled roads, covered in dust.

Never will he touch fodder from another man's meadow.

Coming or going requires no effort — the bull quietly
   carries the man.

3

In patient training the bull got used to the herdsman and is
   truly gentle.

Should he now walk right into dust, he no longer gets dirty.

Long and patient gentling! In one sudden plunge the
   herdsman has won his whole fortune.

Under the trees, others encounter his mighty laugh.

Picture 5

GENTLING THE BULL

Every one of these pictures is significant, and in a way also contains all the others; yet Pictures 5 and 6 are of particular importance. The title of Picture 5 does not seem to match the picture, for surely Picture 4 portrays the gentling of the bull, and here the bull seems already gentled. Are Pictures 4 and 5 then portraying more or less the same thing? Not really — and the clue is in one of the poems to Picture 5, 'Hold the rein tight and do not allow yourself any wavering.' We must never forget that these pictures come from real experience, and so they are remarkably accurate. Once caught, it is not too difficult to constrain the bull somewhat, so that he learns to obey within reason. But that is by no means yet gentled! The real gentling is not the crudeness of just giving in, but is the gentling of the nature itself, and that takes place as portrayed in Picture 5.

What is the difference then? When I was in Japan and talked with American friends about horses, most thought horses somewhat treacherous. It seemed strange, for in Europe horses are not considered treacherous animals. There are many instances of a horse saving its rider. Might there be a difference between a horse being ridden in, and a horse being broken in? You can break in a horse pretty quickly, and it will certainly obey you. Yet given an awkward moment, the horse will get rid of the rider and run off — it is not trustworthy. But a horse that has been properly ridden in will go along willingly with the rider, in the sense that if the rider is incapacitated, the horse will bring him home, will bring him help, will do almost anything.

So there is a process of gentling. Returning to our horse analogy, if broken in too harshly, the spirit may break, and the horse turns either vicious or is just obedient while biding its time. Hence training needs to be gentle, but firm and inexorable — or it cuts no ice! So at first, obedience and giving in have to be learnt or got used to; by that strength of endurance has developed, the strength to carry on in spite of legs hurting, and so on. Now the real gentling process actually starts. This is what is portrayed in Picture 5.

The bull now follows the man. But there is still the rope between them. The text warns, 'If a thought arises, then another inexorably follows it in an endless round.' That in a nutshell states what Zen training is about.

Bodhidharma is said to have brought it from India. 'Acclimatised' in China, it emerged into history after the Sixth Patriarch. There is a seeming paradox concerning the Sixth Patriarch. He is supposed to have run away from the monastery by order of the Fifth Patriarch, on the grounds that there might be contention about the succession. He is supposed also to have been illiterate. Yet in all his talks he shows himself utterly familiar with the most profound Mahayana scriptures, and therefore we can take the story as two-sided, a seeming paradox with which the training continually confronts us. For both sides are always within us; we tend to split and oppose one against the other, instead of realising that both sides need to come together in a merger.

So the Sixth Patriarch is supposed to have been ordered to run away. He was eventually overtaken by a very seasoned old monk. There may then have been a question as to whether he was the genuine successor or merely an impostor who had stolen robe and bowl, the proof of succession. On being overtaken, he put them down on a rock. The pursuer, wanting to possess himself of them, found that he could not lift them. That in itself is a salient point, very much to do with our Picture 5 — Gentling the Bull. Why could he not lift them? A monk's begging bowl and a robe — even if it is the heavy winter robe — can be lifted easily enough. We have to ponder what they represented — the succession — and what they therefore actually meant to the person to whom they were given. They must have meant more than his life. Had his life meant more to him, he would never have been given them! More than his own life, they also represented the rightful inheritance in trust, and with it, the trust to hand it on to the next generation. These constitute values considered above one's own life. All cultures know such values and accordingly honour those who lay down their lives for a value they consider greater.

The Sixth Patriarch must have considered the transmission as above his own life, yet he laid that down, too — placed robe and bowl on a rock. What that really shows is that he laid down everything: his life, his right, his inheritance, his very heart. He had nothing left, and so was at the same place as the Buddha when his five disciples had deserted him because he had taken a bathe and eaten some gruel. Neither prince nor outstanding disciple of a famous teacher, forsaken even by those five, — there was nothing left.

In the Christian representation, this might be analogous to Jesus', 'My God, my God, why hast Thou forsaken me?' Such is the place where there is truly nothing left. Only when all has become truly NOTHING can the change take place, a turning from the delusion of I to the awareness of true nature, the True Face.

Finding that he could not lift robe and bowl, the pursuer, being a seasoned monk of some experience and insight, underwent a sudden change of heart. On just reading the text, the story seems hypocritical. Zen texts frequently present seeming paradoxes — we must look at them with the single eye. The pursuer who had thought that he might face an impostor, now realised that he stood in the presence of the Sixth Patriarch. He very reverently addressed him, 'Elder Brother, I have not come for robe and bowl, I have come for the Dharma.' In a way this was true enough. So the Patriarch asked, 'Before thinking of good and bad, what at that moment is the True Face, before father and mother were born?' And in ourselves, 'Before thinking, what is the True Face?'

If one thought arises, then another inexorably follows on in an endless round. If we want to come to that place where there is really No-thing, then the training must be as the texts say, hard and bitter, because the stripping process towards the place of No-thing is not a pleasant one. It is described as 'breaking one's bones' because that is what it actually feels like. Or breaking one's heart, because the thoughts that follow each other are all undercut when that place of real no-thing-ness suddenly is broken into; and this is necessary for the real gentling of the nature of the bull.

So Picture 5 is called 'Gentling the Bull'. In awakening, everything becomes true; by ignorance it becomes error. The Buddha's insight into the Dharma, the way all things are, constitutes the Buddha's teaching, the Buddha-Dharma. Hence the way all things are and the Buddha-Dharma are not two separate things. The way things really are, is the way things really are. Through ignorance, through delusion, which is our warped seeing, it becomes error because it becomes split into this and that. This is white, isn't it? This is black, it is quite clear. And then we side with this or that, because we pick and choose. This dilemma is portrayed in the early traditional Zen stories, and also what needs to be done about it.

Here the story concerning the succession of the Sixth

Patriarch is helpful. Whoever could compose a verse of sufficient insight would be given the transmission. The old head monk, not certain that he was right, and hence not wanting to be known as the author, at night brushed his poem on a wall: 'The (physical) body is the tree of enlightenment, the heart is like a bright mirror on a stand; the mirror needs to be ever polished so that nothing can becloud it.' But the man who became the Sixth Patriarch, on being told what that verse was about, had his own poem written next to it. 'There is no tree of enlightenment, no bright mirror, and no stand. When there is absolutely nothing, what can becloud what?'

Since we know the author of this second poem became the Sixth Patriarch, we might side with him. We like the idea of a really clean sweep, a new start. So we are already picking and choosing, are we not? But poems like these, teachings like these, are match-pairs; one is not possible without the other. We must not take sides, with one or the other, with either this or that, but need to face both this and that, and realise that the one is necessary for the other to occur; and that the other could occur only because of the one. 'There is something for Buddhas to do, and something for the people to carry out' is such a matched pair. Zen training always presents us with them. We in our ignorance consider them as paradoxes, conundrums, mind-busters — picking and choosing between what this could mean and that might mean, instead of realising that as a pair, we have to see it in the round, from all sides and aspects, clearly and distinctly, but without taking sides, without refusal and without attachment. If we really traverse the place of nothing-at-all, such matched pairs are seen in the round, and we are no longer caught up in thoughts of picking and choosing. The one who thinks, who is he? What happens if there are no more thoughts? What underlies thoughts? That is for us to find out.

'Thoughts arise, not from the surroundings, but out of the herdsman's own heart.' We always think that thoughts are instigated by the surroundings. But they arise from our own heart, according to our reaction pattern. Everything that we remember — or even have forgotten — may come up in our thoughts, instantaneously, when a situation triggers associations. Yet these thoughts cannot be said to come from the situation itself; if there is no outside stimulus, thoughts arise nevertheless, endlessly. Sense deprivation tests have shown that very clearly. If we are not disporting ourselves in outer distractions which stimulate thoughts, then the 'inner film' begins to roll. We do not really need sense deprivation tests to convince ourselves of that; the meditation cushion is good enough! 'One . . . two . . . oh goodness me, when is this going to end?'

I remember a story I heard in Daitoku-ji. A young South African had been sitting there for some months. Then came the hard Rohatsu Sesshin. From the second day on, he could not help it; every period, as soon as it was clapped off, he was outside his home in Cape Town, with his red sports car waiting. He stepped in and drove off, through avenues that he liked most, up this slope which he liked, past those trees which he adored, over this level stretch where he could really go at full speed, all around Table Mountain, and just when, 'ting! ting!' the Inkin sounded again, he arrived back on his cushion!

Not from the surroundings, thoughts arise from one's own heart, even if there is nothing to engender them! They can be dangerous too. In the sixties, when lone sailing first became fashionable, some sailors vanished from their crafts, and others vanished together with their crafts, mostly in calm weather. Questionnaires were circulated to discover why such tragedies occurred, asking what conditions were experienced as the most trying. Surprisingly, the consensus was that while bad weather and storms were, of course, feared, yet there was also a challenge to face. But really scary and frightening to everybody were the long, calm spells where thoughts stretched out all by themselves and existence somehow, too became tenuous. One can quite understand that once this inner film begins to roll, a man may step overboard or become lost with his boat.

Not a thing to be undertaken without a certain amount of training! Some realise this. While training at Daitoku-ji, a young American called. He said he had come to Japan for a specific reason. He was studying mathematics, had two more years to go, but had run out of money. He had so far managed to pay for his study by having a few periods of isolation in a space capsule. Now he had been offered a chance to make sufficient money to pay for the last two years. It entailed being shut up in a space capsule with one other person for some three months. The difficulty was not just being alone, but being crowded with another person. They had been warned that it could get on the nerves! Also, that if they could not stand it for the period the test required and had to be released before, they would forfeit most of the fee! So he had come to learn traditional Zazen to make sure he could endure. I rather liked that; he might not do it for religious reasons, but he had got the essential idea of it. I asked the monastery, and they agreed; he had a good purpose, and if he was willing to go through with it, he would be welcome. He worked hard.

Then he returned to the States, got through the test programme, and completed his degree in mathematics. But, in a strange way, what he had done, sitting it out, both in the monastery and in the space capsule, had given him a feel for the Buddha's Way. After he had got his degree in mathematics, he changed course and read Buddhist philosophy, learning Chinese and Japanese, and qualifying in Buddhist studies and translations. Strange how these things go!

Through awakening, everything becomes truth; through delusion it becomes error. Thoughts arise not from the surroundings, but from the herdsman's own heart. Hold the rein tight, and do not allow yourself any wavering. Thus, the gentling of the bull.

VI — RETURNING HOME ON THE BACK OF THE BULL

Now the struggle is over! Gain and loss, too, have fallen away. The herdsman sings an old folk song or plays a nursery tune on his flute. Looking up into the blue sky, he rides along on the back of the bull. If someone calls after him, he does not look back; nor will he stop if tugged on the sleeve.

POEMS

1

Without haste or hurry, the herdsman rides home on the back
    of the bull.

Far through the evening mist carries the sound of his flute,

Note for note, tune for tune, all carry this boundless mood;

Hearing it, no need to ask how the herdsman feels.

2

Pointing ahead towards the dyke where his home is,

He appears out of mist and fog, playing his flute.

Then suddenly the tune changes to the song of return.

Not even Bai-ya's masterpieces can compare with this song.

3

In bamboo hat and straw coat he rides home through the
    evening mist,

Sitting back to front on the bull, with joy in his heart.

Step by step along in the cool, gentle breeze,

The bull no longer looks at the once irresistible grass.

Picture 6

RETURNING HOME ON THE BACK OF THE BULL

Now to Picture 6. Here the struggle is truly over. The herdsman plays a nursery song on his flute while riding along on the bull. Of the bull it is said that he no longer even looks at the once so alluring grass. The pictures themselves are wonderfully accurate and revealing. Although there is still the rope, it is laid down; there is no more need to guide the bull. The man sits sideways and does not even look into the direction the bull is going. Rather, he plays his flute — not a complicated air, but a folk song, a simple melody that carries them along, step by step. This melody is the 'Song of the Way Home', and so is not a marching song with heavy tread, but rather like a walk on springy turf that lifts one at every step. Look at the picture — this is what it feels like. The nature of the bull has itself become truly gentle, is transformed! This is why the struggle is now over. For the first time, bull and man are really together. They are doubtlessly on the way home.

To begin with, when that pair sets out — and that pair is in each one of us — we have ideas about the bull, and are convinced the bull has to be ridden or driven in the direction I want to go. I want to go home and so I have to guide the bull. Also, I would love to know the way home and I would love to ride that bull; but the fact is, I cannot do so. Usually the bull wins by one ploy or another and carries me away. Or I become so rigid that the life goes out of the bull, and I become ill. Hence training, gentling the bull is essential; for only the bull knows the way home, and only he has the strength to carry the man there.

Looking at any standard representation or picture of the Wheel of Change, with its six states, it is held in the claws of a demon — actually it is subject to change, which I see as a demon. 'Parting from what one likes and not having what one likes' and so on — what I see as a demon is but the flow of nature, coming to be, existing and ceasing to be. There is nothing to be frightened about, nothing to be resisted. The six states on the Wheel are the human state, that of heavenly beings, of fighting demons, of hungry ghosts, of miserable beings in the hells and of animals that have to take whatever is meted out to them by their surroundings and by us humans!

Now, though we have human bodies, very rarely do we inhabit the human state. For how many hours a day do we transmigrate through all the other states? For how many hours a day do we abide in the human state, true human beings — without delusion, without wanting, without anger; not feeling I am the centre. One could therefore say that at Picture 6, when the bull has been gentled, the human state has been truly entered for the first time.

The pair have become truly human; even the bull, now transformed, gentled, does not graze out of the human state any more. So he carries the man home. This is the important thing and is what the gentling of the bull is about.

Here the true human being has been 'formed', and can now unfold, no longer merely biologically but culturally, which is the human prerogative. The Confucian 'gentleman', or with us the 'true gentleman' in the best sense of the word, it comes to the same thing. In the gentled man his nature is itself gentled, not just a veneer of outside manners with wildness still raging inside. Only when the nature itself has been so gentled can the human state prevail, under all circumstances, good, bad or indifferent. When courtesy, good manners and all the other attributes which go to make up this truly human state truly prevail always and of themselves, they are realised as coming from the heart, qualities of the human heart. Are we becoming a bit clearer about what this heart-bull actually represents and why we must labour, suffer and endure in this gentling or humanising process, this great endeavour? As to 'good form', therefore, if cultivated only as a veneer, sheep's skin to hide the wolf, then we do well to distrust it. But the form-giving aspect of good and gentle manners used for that cultivation, the gentling of wild nature, is what education is about. Mere cramming full of knowledge is a poor substitute. For only when truly gentled in our nature can we live in peace and harmony with ourselves and each other, and can we begin to understand ourselves and so each other.

Thus Picture 6 presents a crucial stage in our training. In a way it is the state which living beings born in a human body are supposed to be in. We are perhaps not quite that far developed, though we have human bodies. So there is need first to become true human beings, because of all the states on the Wheel, only from the human one is deliverance possible. Hence the all-importance of the human state, and the constant encouragement not to waste such a rare opportunity. For not even from the state of heavenly beings can deliverance be attained. When the good Karma that has resulted in temporary residence in that state eventually wears out, as wear out it does, signs of decline begin to appear. These are graphically described as sweat collecting under the armpits; the flowers they carry begin to wither; the beautiful, shining robes that they have worn without ever having to launder, take on grime and begin to smell. Not only is there no 'better' state on the Wheel of Change, but in all the joyous and innocent life of that state there has been no chance to accumulate any merit. So when the good Karma that brought them there is exhausted, down they go, perhaps even to the miserable states — depending on the residue of Karma, and the endless round on the Wheel continues. From the human state only is deliverance possible.

Birth in a human body is a rare and precious opportunity, not to be wasted. We do well to give ourselves into the training. If there is the additional good Karma of the Buddha's teaching, and of getting to know what is at stake, we may master sufficient energy to work on our humanisation rather than continue in our old unregenerate habits of picking and choosing, of quarrelling and fighting with each other for this and that. Though the body is human, only when the bull is gentled, only when the energy of the afflicting passions is transformed from 'elemental fire' to 'human', only then is the human state a place of residence in which the Way of the Buddha now beckons the human being.

All religions recognize the true human being as an all-important stage and work towards it. If one really looks at it, one could say that religious practices are first oriented towards humanisation, until there is a full human being; and from then on the truly religious way begins, though it has seemed a religious way from the beginning. So there are two decisive stages. The first one, which is concerned with the gentling of the bull, starts with a practice of genuinely laying down and becoming nothing, until the bull himself is gentle, so human that he now goes 'home' into the fully human state and carries the man with him. Home is beckoning, and the man does not need to guide the bull. This is the natural rhythm of 'going home', no impatience, no I must, no nothing — just a true at-one-ment in the moment. This is what we begin to cultivate with the very first step of our training, giving ourselves as well as possible into what is being done now. Step by step on that way home, it comes to completion.

The text of one of the poems to Picture 6 says that the bull walks in the direction of the dyke. Home beckons, and suddenly the melody changes and becomes a song of return. To one capable of hearing it, even the greatest poem seems no longer outstanding. To hear that song of return is more beautiful, and it is also more heart-warming, than any other. With the heart thus being touched, 'warming', we begin to realise where the Way leads. Until now, there was the work with the bull, there was the laying down, there was the hard and bitter training; and behind all that there was still desire, I want. Without that want, we could never have set out; without that desire we could not have continued walking. This is called the aspiration of the heart, or the strength of the vow of dedication. Though essential, yet it is still desire; in the end, that too needs to be laid down. The question is how to lay down that which is the most precious thing.

This is encountered in full only late in the training, yet to some degree it is demanded at almost every step. Why is it so very important? The passions are the Buddha-Nature and the Buddha-Nature is the passions. Suppose I want something very much. At some stage in our life we all have wanted something desperately and felt that if only we could have it, or keep it, we would be happy ever after. I may have had the misfortune of actually getting it — not for long, for nothing is for ever — but for a time. So we all have the experience that even if I get what I so much wanted, it does not really give me the fulfilment I expected; it begins to pale almost at once. Even worse, I now have nothing to strive for that promises happiness ever after. Whatever that something might be, a concrete thing, a person, or an abstract idea, the 'bond' of my wanting, my irresistible fascination with the desired object, comes about by a projection of my own heart, my 'heart's desire'. Remember the golden ball rolling away? Or the heart jumps out and drapes itself over an object which now exerts an irresistible fascination. Then, mistaking the object for my own heart, I cannot but feel that if I only can incorporate it, I will be whole, fulfilled. But we also know that familiarity breeds contempt, and sooner or later, as I become acquainted with the coveted object, the veil which is my heart thins and drops away. When I now see the object as it is, there is disappointment, for it is not what I wanted! Might it be my own heart that I 'want' and need to be aware of for feeling whole and fulfilled? Thus my heart jumps out from time to time to make me aware, 'You blockhead, look at me! This is what you really want! I am your own heart, your True Face! Don't mistake me for outside objects. Just look, and say yes.'

In fact, we need to have quite a few experiences of how that shimmering heart-veil drapes itself over an object, only to fade again in due course. It happens to me, I do not, and indeed cannot, make it happen by an act of will. We fall in love, don't we? Can you make yourself fall in love with a person, an idea, or the training?

As the Daily Life Practice fosters awareness, the repeated experiences of this process at last bring it home to the blockhead I am that it is my own heart which so irresistibly draws me, and what is needful is to come together with this my own heart, not with the object.

Now we can look again at the simple and well-known 'I want something'. The fascination that seems to cling to the object is really my own heart or heart-bull! With this clearer seeing we can disengage from the object, refrain from making pictures and mistaking them for our heart's desire. So from 'I want something', I am now left with a truncated 'I want'! It is now seen that this want is of a power that is well-nigh irresistible, ready and wanting to form itself into a picture and compelling me to go after it. This is why all the developed religions warn against making graven images, concrete or abstract concepts. 'The Tao that can be named is not the eternal Tao.' What, in the Southern Tradition, did the Buddha say on his awakening? 'Now I have seen you, builder of the house; the ridge-pole is broken, never shall you build new houses again.' We need not interpret these houses as from life to life; this life is good enough. The new houses are then the pictures that we continuously paint, or rather that paint themselves, on an inherently empty mirror — trails of thoughts, one arising with another following in an endless round! I live in this imaginary world of pictures, and feel I need them, for without them and without having to chase after them, I have nothing to do, actually am nothing — a prospect dimly suspected and filling me with terror!

If both — the terror of becoming nought, and the primal strength which is in the imperative 'want' — can be endured without another escape into picture-formations, that is experiencing 'I want' in its primal strength or power. Energy is dynamic, and work it must. Prevented from going into the making of pictures and chasing after them, it turns round, and seemingly attacks what is still there — 'I'. If there is enough strength truly to open up at least in small ways, and rather than resisting the energy, invite it, 'Yes, work on me', then a burning and churning results until what is still there — I — is burnt and churned away, and so the energy is purified and transformed because there is no-thing left. At the moment when there is nothing, when I am not there to observe or to judge, the energy has reverted again to what it always has been — the Buddha-Nature. For this transformation to take place, the gentling of the bull is a necessary condition. The gentled bull is the strength that arises, phoenix-like, from the burning Fires. And this purification, or deliverance from the force of delusive pictures, is portrayed as the gentled bull carrying the man home.

For all these seemingly manifold reasons — which are fundamentally just the true gentling of the wildness of the heart

— working with the bull, that is patient endurance and determined continuation of practice, are absolutely essential. If the heart really wants to go that Way, it is possible for it to do so without being distracted or deluded by all the thought-forms that usually trail around and veil what really is. So, looking neither left nor right, riding on the gentled bull and playing the flute, the man is both at one with the bull, and at one with the playing, and therefore is free. Can you remember what is said of the unregenerate bull? 'Stubborn self-will rages in him and wild animal nature rules him'. No longer here. In Picture 6 he has truly been gentled, transformed. The energy is certainly not lost or vanished, but has now become the purified carrying power that flows in the direction of home, a steady strength that also knows the way home. Although home is everywhere, and already beckons, the actual way of return is a long one, and demands undivided strength and aspiration to bridge the gulf between the whole human being and the spirit.

For that, two further stages are necessary. Bull and man, not only acting as one and being in harmony, actually have to become one (Picture 7), and then there must be a complete and unconditional laying down (Picture 8). Since this does not take place of itself, much further training is necessary, which now we can consider as the 'religious way' proper that goes beyond the fully human towards the spirit. So the training goes on and on and on. Though with each stage comes a feeling of 'this is it', there is a true 'this is it' from the very first step on; those who have been training for a long time are fully aware of it, and so also of inertia which is part of all matter, and always whispers, 'This is it,' and wants to settle down and go no further. Remember 'Mara's temptations'! That is where the Buddha's teaching of compassion helps us. True compassion starts with ourselves; but as I become less focussed on 'I only', it quite naturally spreads out to encompass others.

There are thus many grades of compassion. In the beginning

it acts as a spur when we repeat the four great vows. To an outsider it may seem presumptuous or hypocritical to dare to make such vows, but their significance becomes clear in the process of training. Even the first steps can be taken only by virtue of the power of a vow. If the vow is not truly in the heart as an aspiration, I will inevitably settle down on the very first stage, if indeed I have managed to bestir myself to start walking at all.

VII — BULL FORGOTTEN — MAN REMAINS

There are not two Dharmas. Provisionally only has the bull been set up, somewhat in the nature of a sign-post. He might also be likened to a snare for catching rabbits, or to a fishing net. Now the herdsman feels as when the shining gold has been separated out from the ore, or as when the moon appears from behind a cloud bank. The one cool light has been shining brilliantly since the time before the beginning.

POEMS

1

The herdsman has come home on the back of the bull.

Now the bull is forgotten and the man is at ease.

He may still sleep though the hot sun stands high in
mid-heaven.

Whip and rein are now useless and thrown away under
the eaves.

2

Though the herdsman has brought the bull down from the
mountain, the stable is empty.

Straw coat and bamboo hat, too, have become useless.

Not bound by anything, and at leisure, singing and dancing,

Between heaven and earth he has become his own master.

3

Now the herdsman has returned, home is everywhere.

When both things and self are wholly forgotten, peace reigns
all day long.

Believe in the peak 'Entrance to the Deep Secret' —

No man can settle on this peak's summit.

Picture 7

BULL FORGOTTEN, MAN REMAINS

The remaining Pictures 7 to 10 are best taken as pointers. The truly religious way in — but no longer entirely of — the human world, starts with Picture 7. The caption reads, 'Bull Forgotten — Man Remains'. But the bull is not just forgotten; he has 'gone into change', is transformed. As bull he has gone for good; the herdsman remains. Where has the bull vanished to? To forget something is one thing; but here the bull himself, in his nature, has become human, at one with the herdsman. And as the whole human heart, thus fulfilled and completed, lifts up, the erstwhile herdsman now sits on a mountain peak in front of a little hermitage. In this place there is only one gesture possible, one which is both human and spiritual, and that is kneeling down with folded hands and looking up towards the 'high'. If we have nothing to look up to, if nothing is above ourselves, then I myself care too little and so the heart cannot open. There is always more than myself, and this is what with shining eyes and open heart the herdsman, whose heart is now the living bull become completely human, looks up to. Never think you have arrived; however far it may seem up the mountain, it is but a ledge to sit down on and catch one's breath. There is always a higher place if one looks up, and if one looks down, there is a lot to be done!

It can be very beguiling to think that I am now on top. But the one who is capable of saying or thinking that is as yet far below. On that peak one looks up and sees what more is above! That is important to realise.

Also important is that on a par with the higher mountain peak is not the sun, but the moon. The texts always refer to the brilliant, icy moon. There is a reason for that too. If the whole of the Buddhist training is about gentling the bull, of transforming the energy that flares up as the compulsion of the afflicting passions, then it is rather dangerous to compare that with the hot sun. So the brilliant, icy cold winter moon is the usual symbol for being free of the afflicting passions. Not 'hot', and its light different from sunlight with its sharp contrasts and dark shadows, it shows up differences, yet without sharp contrasts. That is how we see by the light of the full moon, whereas the sun casts heavy shadows in a world of dualism. There I cannot help but take sides and just there I come in.

This mountain peak is said to be the 'Entrance to the Deep Secret', and also that it is not a place for humans to settle down. Come to it we must, but settling there is not possible; it is either going further along the Way of the Buddha, or stagnating and falling back. For though the bull has really vanished, the man must abdicate, let go of himself on that peak and dedicate himself to the Way, to the religious, the spiritual life. Just as in Picture 6 the trammels of I have been transcended and the True Human Being freed, so in Picture 7 even that is transcended and must be transcended to make the next step — to Picture 8 — possible. 'The Buddha Way is supreme; I vow to go it to the end.' Picture 7 portrays the inner landscape of this vow. So there is a very real change, a very real dedication, and then walking on.

But there is still another and most significant point to be

considered. Picture 7, 'Bull Forgotten, Man Remains', also illustrates the dire need for the real gentling of the bull. Not just on the surface only, but an inner, in-depth transformation of the bull nature. 'Bull Vanished, Man Remains.' If the training has not been thorough enough, not been hard and bitter, with no bones broken, what happens? The change goes the opposite way, 'Man Forgotten, Bull Remains'. We have all at one stage or another come across bull men or bull women, in the family or at the office. But these are the minor ones only. The full extent of the calamitous power of such bull possession may be studied in secular and religious history.

To make sure of the bull being really gentled, ordinary daily life is our training ground. It provides ample opportunity to check and recheck whether there still is even the slightest of rearings. If so, firmly on with the training, more training and yet more training!

I remember Sesso Roshi, under whom I had the good fortune to train for six years, telling me that his teacher, Zuigan Roshi, who lived to a very old age, was what the Zen tradition, with great respect and admiration, calls 'a severe teacher'. Every month Sesso Roshi went to visit Zuigan Roshi, and naturally always took his attendant monk with him. This office of attendant to the Roshi is, as are all other offices, for half a year, and is a very formative time. In a Rinzai monastery, the Roshi is not considered a 'Guru', but without him there to give Sanzen interviews and Teisho talks, there would be neither Rinzai training nor guidance. Hence the importance and deference accorded him, for his well-being is of paramount importance to the community, and all regard him with trust and respect. There is no reason to stay if that is not there. The attendant monk, therefore, has to study the Master's idiosyncrasies, and for the half year of his office, makes the Master's well-being his own, forgetting himself. Hence the importance and formative effect of this office — and the set period of duration so that the formation can take place, but not long enough to become too personal; the latter is strictly discouraged.

Anyway, back to the story. I knew from a succession of monks that they loathed Sesso Roshi's visits to Zuigan Roshi. Sesso Roshi was a mild and mellow Master whom one could not help but respect and revere. But Zuigan Roshi — in their presence — treated Sesso Roshi as if he were a first year monk.

Sesso Roshi told me, and I have never forgotten it, 'I know the monks hate it. But I can't tell you what it does to me! Here I am, Roshi, Lord-Abbot of Daitoku-ji. All I hear is , "Yes, Sir;" "Sir, if you wish it so," from everyone I come into contact with; nothing else. It is a very lonely position. Then once a month, when I visit Zuigan Roshi, I feel young again. I am so grateful; he still treats me like a raw beginner! Seeing they are upset, I try to convey that to my attendants. They do not really understand, but they will find out in due course.'

That really is the test, is it not? If I feel threatened in circumstances that belittle or diminish me, if there is the slightest quiver, then there is a great deal of training still necessary. Actually such tests do occur, not only in the normal training or daily life situations, but the Roshi occasionally begins to 'fish'. Suddenly an accusation is thrown at one, obviously trumped up. In the beginning there is a flicker, 'What are you blaming me for?' Then one goes away smarting and feeling, 'I must set it right, I must make him understand.' By the time that has gone on for a year or two, the realisation dawns that it does not really matter. It is not one's business. One begins to remember training stories, like that of Master Hakuin who, when wrongly accused of a really great misdemeanour by the whole village, just commented, 'Is that so?' There was no trying to wash himself white although he was certainly not guilty. Just saying, 'Is that so?' and leaving it at that. When the situation changed and his innocence became known, leaving it at that too;

his only comment again, 'Is that so?'

Or that other story already mentioned of the early Chinese master who was ostracised and banished to a mountain peak. There he taught the bears and the wolves and the stones. Then he was asked back again, and that was also all right. This is going with circumstances as they are, without having to take any personal issue at all. When that has become transparent and clear, then No-I has passed the 'Entrance to the Deep Secret'. No-I can sit on that mountain peak; and in any case, No-I has no place to sit down even for a short while; therefore there is no temptation to remain on that mountain peak! No-I realises that there is actually no such place, that there is no realisation and no temptation to sit down either. Even if there were such a place, No-I, being nothing at all, cannot sit down anyway!

All these meanings are pointed at in the picture. From Picture 7 we are faced with religious pictures that point but are not meant to be 'grasped'. What they point at is a mystery. From the side of I, a mystery cannot be understood, cannot be grasped; it can only be revered. In the act of reverence, bowing deeply before it, the heart may open. Thus open, it may reflect the mystery, and, with continuing training, partake in it.

After I had been training under him for some two or three years, Master Sesso occasionally allowed me to come and make up the ink for his calligraphy. One day, the moment I appeared on the threshold and bowed, he said, 'You know, what is really important cannot be translated at all.' I had just been confronted by difficulties of translations, especially of the old stories, because though they are freely told, and generally very freely rendered, it is by people who know what they are about. So I said, 'Yes,' and thought how glad I was that this had been truly emphasised. The Roshi looked at me and said, 'No, no. You do not really understand. What is most important cannot be translated.' I thought of the Koans, — all have got what technically is called an 'eye' and if that does not come across or is slanted, the Koan or 'case' loses its point, though on the surface it is still the same story. I thought, yes, that is an important point. 'Fool! What is really important cannot be translated!' Having seen in my face my mistaken grasping at an idea of mine, Sesso Roshi cited an example. Though Japanese, its sense is readily accessible to us too. 'Just think of going to worship at a Shinto shrine. There is the grid where you place your offering. Then you pull at the straw rope with the little bell on top. The bell summons the deity (Kami) so that it may come out of its little house up there and reveal itself to the worshipper who then folds his hands and bows in the Presence.' Sesso Roshi suddenly smiled and continued, 'It is irrelevant whether the deity is there or not; it cannot be seen anyway! But what happens in the heart of the sincere believer as he deeply bows in the Presence, that is the blessing — and that cannot be translated!'

We need to bear that in mind when we approach the religious realm, when we see Pictures like 7 to 10, hear or read stories which to us are mysteries; they are to be revered, not to be understood. If I think I can understand them, I have put them simply into the category of 'Oh, yes, nothing but...', and with that have lost the whole impact. The mystery is gone, the heart closes up and feels desolate.

Laurens van der Post tells a Zulu story. A herdsman had some beautiful cows and he loved every one of them. One morning he found that they did not give any milk. He was rather unhappy and thought he had mistaken their grazing; so he was very careful to put them to good pasture that day. However, the next morning they were again without milk. He was most upset and went to enormous trouble to find them luscious grazing, anticipating what amount of frothing, creamy milk he would get; but next morning they were again dry. He began to feel suspicious and in the evening, he corralled the cows and hid himself to watch. At about midnight, ladders came down from the sky, and a whole flock of heavenly maidens swarmed down, each with a little calabash on her arm. They began milking the cows, then drank the milk and made merry, dancing about. Angrily he rushed from his hiding place. 'You are stealing my milk! What are you doing to my cows?' But they all quickly climbed the ladders again and pulled them up. All except one maiden, who was too far away and could not reach a ladder in time. The cowherd grabbed her. 'What have you done to my cows?' Suddenly he realised how beautiful she was, and said, 'Now you are going to stay here and be my wife.' The maiden answered, 'I will stay, and I will bring you fortune and happiness and increase. There is only one condition. My little calabash — never, never, never must you look into it. It contains good fortune for both of us.' So the little calabash with its lid was put on the window sill, and they lived happily for a time. The cows thrived and everything prospered.

Under such circumstances inevitably the calabash began to exert an irresistible attraction. The cowherd could not help it; ever more he felt he must know what was in it. He tried to keep his promise, but one day the attraction was too strong. His wife was out with the cows, so he stealthily approached the window sill, and lifting the lid a trifle, cautiously peered inside — and burst out laughing. There was nothing in it! He laughed and laughed and laughed. In the evening, when his wife came back, he was still laughing. She realised what had happened, and cried out, 'What did you do?' He, still laughing, said, 'Oh you woman, you silly woman! Why have you made such a song and dance about that calabash? There is nothing in it!' She burst out crying. 'You have allowed our happiness together to fly away; now there is nothing left, and I must go away.' She took the calabash which had seemed empty, and putting it over her arm, left, going towards the sunset, and was never seen again.

That 'nothing but' — if we want to see, if we want to grasp, to possess ourselves of and to hold with our little ignorant mind the contents of the calabash, or of the Buddhist teachings, and think we understand! If we look thus at a mystery, it runs away to 'nothing but' and we become mean and shallow. So from our side, in front of the mystery there is only one move or gesture — a bow. Then possibly for a moment, the heart lights up and reflects it, beckoning us onto the mountain peak. If we have worked enough and the gentled bull has vanished, has become human — not just forgotten but transformed to human stature — the calamity of becoming a bull man or a bull woman cannot befall us. The bowing is then the confirmation of the entrance to the peak, of the Deep Secret, on which there is no place for human folk to settle down — because it is not a place.

So, without settling down, where does the next step go? There is no end; and the man is still here. There is but one thing which is not yet known to him. The texts also state clearly what is necessary to follow the Buddha's path, and they also list the difficulties for us and say what needs to be laid down — I. But I has very deep roots. An individuality, or whatever suits 'me', or what might be possible for me though not possible for you, all these need to be laid down. Then there are still some remnants — there is a being, a living being that also needs to be laid down. Finally what needs to be laid down so that the whole root of I is uplifted, is a life.

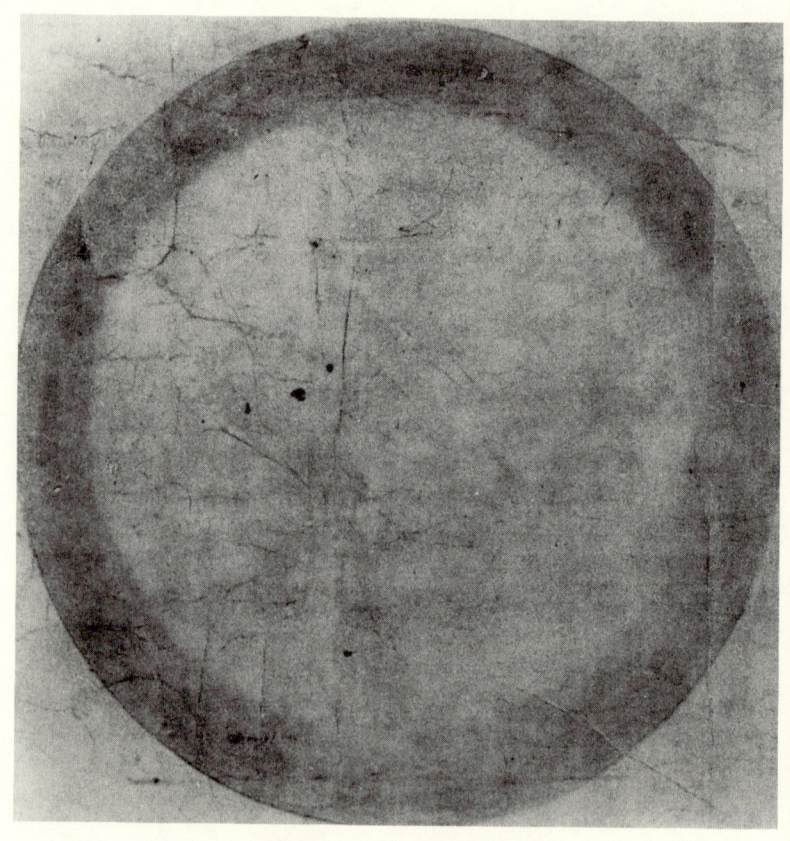

VIII — BOTH BULL AND MAN FORGOTTEN

When all worldly wanting dropped away, holiness, too, lost its meaning. Do not stay at a place where Buddha is, and pass quickly by where he is not. If one remains unattached to either, not even a thousand eyes can spy him out. Holiness to which birds consecrate flowers is shameful.

POEMS

1

Whip and rein, bull and man, are all gone and vanished.

No words can encompass the blue vault of the sky.

How could snow pile up on a red-hot hearth?

Only when arrived at this place can a man match the old masters.

2

Shame! Up till now I wanted to save the whole world;

Now, surprise! There is no world to be saved!

Strange! Without ancestors or successors,

Who can inherit, who pass on this truth?

3

Space shattered at one blow and holy and worldly both vanished.

In the Untreadable the path has come to an end.

The bright moon over the temple and the sound of wind in
the tree,

All rivers, returning their waters, flow back again to the sea.

Picture 8

MAN AND BULL BOTH FORGOTTEN

For that 'laying down of a life' in Picture 7 there leads the passage to what Master Hakuin calls the Great Death portrayed as an empty circle, because death is not yet known. Moreover, death — not only of I but of everything, entering the voidness of no-thing at-all — is not yet known in Picture 7. Picture 8 hints at that. 'Man and Bull Both Forgotten', gone without trace! Not as concepts, of course, that is of no use; but to be taken as a pointer to a mystery. All religions have such pointers or representations. With regard to that empty circle, we might think that in Christianity this is represented by the Passion of Christ and the Crucifixion — the voiding of every-thing, from 'Why hast thou forsaken me?' to 'Into thy hands I commend my spirit.'

To us, death is the great unknown, a mystery we fear. The reasons for this fear are not far to seek. We have no religious values left that set limits to this fear by 'showing' another picture. The analogy of wave and ocean, if we know it at all, makes at best an intellectual impact but is certainly not the living awareness that pervades all thinking and doing.

Nowadays we somehow tend to feel that we know, or at least

ought to know, everything. But what makes us so cock-sure that everything is 'knowable'? We are only too prone to sneer at others who still 'have not found' a cure for this or that. But we seem incapable of considering that it just might conceivably be our own stubbornness, greed, delusion and total incapability of any restraint, which produced 'this and that' — indeed we would hotly deny that we ourselves fashioned such things by our own unbridled conduct. Our own 'considered', that is hot, opinions and wants ride us — stubbornness rages and wild animal nature rules, as the text says of the bull. So we demand rights without accepting any duties. And even if we think we are taking up some altruistic cause, before we know where we are, we are already marching for peace, fighting for this or that right, and engaged in some destructive or violent demonstration. We cannot help it, cannot help ourselves, because we are divided inside ourselves and hence one-sided, incapable of taking in both sides. We are too narrow because fear shrinks us. Yet, without having made peace in our own heart, there can be no peace outside either.

These days we know a lot — mostly in the head only. Hence our knowledge is mostly about things — how something is, how it works, but not what it is — the latter is in itself unknowable, though we flatter ourselves that we 'know'. And yet, we do not know what LIFE is, for we cannot make it, cannot enliven an inanimate form, for example. Helpful for such considerations is to realize that LIFE as such is not; it is merely a concept. It does not exist by itself, without forms. Neither does Death as such. We believe we know LIFE; and in a way we do, for we live it. But of death that awaits us all, we know nothing; and we fear that unknown, the state of I not being.

Since we have lost most, if not all, our religious and cultural values and so willy-nilly are regressed to only value 'myself' and 'my' opinions (or 'ours', our side, which comes to the same), fear of death has greatly increased. This is further exacerbated by the media ceaselessly reporting violence and death by violence, representing death in its most gory forms. We may all have witnessed traffic accidents, if not worse, and yes, they are pitiful and tragic.

But who nowadays has not only seen, but actually been with, a dying person, cared and looked after an old parent or relative? And at the end seen the dignity and majesty of a dead face, died in peace? If that would still be general 'knowledge' in the sense of general experience — and such dying the rule rather than the exception — we might perhaps be less afraid of death. But we conveniently shove our elderly relatives away into hospital or old people's homes because we cannot be bothered with caring for them as we are too busy and have no time to spare. This selfishness robs us of an essential human experience, and so imagination roams instead, and fear grows. We are not quite unaware of this; but again, delusion deceives us. There is much talk about caring these days — care about all kinds of abstract, general issues — apt to lead to aggression and violence as such issues do. And the 'caring professions' are much to the fore; but laudable as they are, are they genuine? I may go and take care of some old person, with my own mother in a home! For thus, I only take care for some hours, perhaps all 'my' working time; usually I am also trained how to take care. So I am quite unaware that I now arrogantly assume I know how to take care of you and you jolly well cooperate and appreciate it — and after my stint with you is over, I go home and have a respite from it all with good conscience. Thus I have not really given anything, only increased my self-esteem.

But to take care of somebody at home, who is there all the time, that is really giving, and it allows little if any respite, nor will I be able to maintain a condescending attitude of 'I know and you cooperate'. The problems are very real, and show clearly how little bearing-tolerance we have when faced with such a situation. Or, when it comes down to it, how little we really have to give. Hence also how little prepared we are to face death.

Another aspect connected with fear and death is positively encouraged today and so adds greatly to the whole syndrome. If I feel an urge (uprush of emotional energy, of afflicting passion; in short of the bull) there is little that gives me pause, helps me to consider and restrain myself. Rather, I am told it is natural to express 'myself', to gratify myself or whatever. Consequently we never cultivate inner or moral strength, and so have little if any to hold us up in adversity. The result is that I can only act when 'fired', that is can do or act only when prompted by greed for gain or fame, or I need either a challenge or an issue that constellates group-emotion to supply energy for action. 'By myself' I drift like a rudderless ship — a condition that is particularly assailing younger people. Though the longings are there as of old, yet in fact, and because of this lack of available energy, I have little to give, and so fear of death is increasing. Language often gives very clear hints; perhaps the only taboo word today is 'death' — just that.

So Picture 8 presents to us a fearsome and feared mystery; a true handing over without any reservation, a willing going with whatever may befall, an unconditional surrender. Parallel to it is a Zen Buddhist parable by Master Kyogen. He knew what he was talking about; he had himself gone through something like this, as all great masters have, not just mentally but in their own bodies. Master Kyogen's analogy for the state of Picture 8 is a man hanging on a perpendicular cliff. He has slithered down it, one hand just grabbing a root. There he now hangs, by one hand; the other hand and both legs dangle over that precipice. Can he now let go and plummet into the abyss? Life certainly hangs us onto that precipice, at least a few times, but we do not recognise it, do we? Nor do we know what to do on that precipice. With toes and fingernails we struggle to climb up again, and since we are here, we have succeeded in doing so!

Life is the ideal training yard, but it does not always tell us what to do, or we refuse to listen. Since we thus remain ignorant, delusion — the first link in the twelve-fold chain of Dependent Origination — is strong in all of us. We do not know what to do when life presents us with options. So we need to do a training which in a way would seem quite unnecessary; but there is no other way. Training, too, kicks us yelling over that cliff. Furious at the training which does such nasty things to us, we scramble back up, only to be kicked over once more! Cruel? Why be kicked down instead of being put right onto that mountain peak where I would like to go and settle down? Away from it all! 'I' would! But training, if it is thorough, will not only kick us over that cliff, it will also tell us what we need to do — and why — when we hang on that cliff; and it tells us what the root is on which we hang — that one thing we feel we must have, or get rid of, that one thing which would suffice, and I would be content. A proverb says, 'The healthy man has a thousand wants. The really sick has only one.'

So when everything in our life once more comes down to that 'one thing only', as it has no doubt done at least a few times, when nothing else matters but that one thing — whatever it might be — that is the root on which we dangle over the precipice. My heart is given to that one thing, so much that I feel I cannot live without it! To open my hand and let go of the root, feels truly like suicide. But once 'de-clutched' from the 'thing', from the root — wonder of wonders! — not death at all from loss of heart, rather the heart is discovered as having been there all the time, never 'lost outside'.

Opening the hand that clutches the root is what training teaches us to do! To repeat, life hangs us on the precipice a few times; and training certainly kicks us over that precipice. That is what we are doing it for. But it also tells us what the root is so that we may recognise it when we hang on it, and it teaches us how to let go of it. In long and hard and bitter training, sufficient strength is developed to open the hand and, though everything in me shrieks, to let go. But no training, not even Buddha, can actually prise that hand open; that is what I myself must do, and hurtle down the cliff, right into no-thing-ness. Yes, it does feel like death. Master Hakuin calls it the Great Death, that is died to Life. So can we possibly say there is the entrance to the Great Life? Can we imagine it? Of course we cannot. We can only reflect, again and again, that this is where the training will lead; and prepare ourselves so as to be able to recognise that root. We do the training so as to make ourselves — I with my likings and loathings — ever smaller, so that our demands are shrinking and the weight that hangs on the root is not too heavy for us to open the hand.

When Master Kyogen hung on that root, there was very little of him left. He had seemingly shipwrecked quite early in his training. When hardly out of his teens, his teacher, under whom he had been for only a couple of years, died. His successor, the former head monk Issan, knew young Kyogen as brilliant and of great potential, but as yet dazzled by his own brilliance. So when, as customary, Kyogen begged to be allowed to continue under him, Issan tested him, saying, 'Are you sure you wish to continue, having already learned all the Sutras by heart?' Kyogen was pleased to be recognised, and replied, 'A year or two more would certainly help.' 'You conceited young fool,' scolded the teacher, 'do you think that all the Sutras in the world will make you understand the real mystery? Where do you go after death? Do you know?'

You see, we come back to death again and again. Anyway, the young Kyogen was convinced that every answer was to be found in the Scriptures. Since he knew them all by heart, one can imagine how they all rattled through his mind as he searched for 'Where do I go when dead?' But however he searched, he could not find the answer on the spot. Rather perturbed, he admitted that he could not recall it just now and could he be excused to go and look it up? He searched through all the Sutras, volumes and volumes, hundreds of fascicles. Days passed, but nowhere did he find the answer. More and more upset and perturbed, but with unshaken conviction that somewhere in the Sutras there would be the answer to the question, he forgot sleeping and eating for days. In a minor way, we all know such a state — being really gripped by something, compelled so that we cannot let go. Having reviewed all the Sutras to no avail, Kyogen was now in real doubt and unbearable confusion. He rushed to Master Issan. 'I cannot find the answer in the Sutras. Please tell me! I cannot bear it any longer, please!' Issan said, 'It cannot be told, nor would I rob you of finding out for yourself.' Kyogen, not having eaten or slept for several days and being worked up to breaking point, lost control and grabbed his teacher, threatening, 'You must tell me — I cannot continue otherwise. Tell or I kill you!' In that state, he meant it. Master Issan, though doubtlessly aware of the reality of the threat, yet roared with laughter. 'And do you think that my dead body is going to tell you?'

At that, deflated like a pricked balloon, Kyogen became himself again. He realised what he had done, that he had laid violent hands on his Master; realised, too, the consequence — for this life he had lost all possible affinity links with the teachings. He sincerely apologised, and took respectful leave of the Master. It seemed to him that the only thing to do (he was only 21 at the time) was somehow to spend his life as harmlessly as possible and firmly to resolve that in his next life he would take up the training again, or in the following one, but that he would continue walking the Buddha's Path. So he wandered about as an itinerant monk, just biding his time. After some ten years, chance, if you want to call it so, brought him to the tomb of the Sixth Patriarch, which at that time was neglected and unattended. Kyogen stayed and kept the place weeded, swept and cleaned, feeling he might as well spend his life being useful in that way.

Another ten years passed. Then one day when as always he was sweeping the yard and collecting leaves and the odd pebble in his trug, as he emptied it into the bamboo thicket, one pebble happened to click against a bamboo trunk, a usual enough occurrence. But at that moment the time was ripe — the click did not go into Kyogen's ears only, but went right into his heart! In the analogy of hanging over the cliff, the hand opened because there was nothing there that could hold on, nor anything that could be held on to! He hurtled through that empty circle, and realised Great Satori. In his own poem composed on the occasion, he describes how he put away his tools, bathed, and for the first time in twenty years put on his full monk's robes again. He went up a little hill and in the direction of far away Issan made nine full prostrations in gratitude to his teacher who even at the peril of his life did not rob him of his own realisation of passing through that empty circle, had not robbed him of himself dying the Great Death that needs to be died in order to awaken to the Great Life which is not 'mine'.

So these last four pictures are to be seen as pointers to mysteries which help us to bow and to revere. Even in a spiritual ice-age such as ours, they help us to open the heart in reverence, in gratitude to something which we do not know and which in itself is nothing, but which lives in all of us and 'in-forms' us. Unless we revere it, it will never touch us with its bliss-bestowing hands, and so cannot point to the next step that now needs to be taken.

IX — RETURN TO THE ORIGIN, BACK TO THE SOURCE

In the origin all is pure and there is no dust. Collected in the peace of non-volitional doing (Wu-Wei) he beholds the coming and going of all things. No longer deluded by shifting phantom pictures, he has nothing further to learn. Blue runs the river, green range the mountains; he sits by himself and beholds the change of all things.

POEMS

1

Returned to the origin, back at the source, all is completed.

Nothing is better than suddenly being as blind and deaf.

Inside his hermitage, he does not look out.

Boundless, the river runs as it runs. Red bloom the flowers
  just as they bloom.

2

The great activity does not pander to being or not being.

And so, to see and to hear he need not be as one deaf
  and blind.

Last night the golden bird flew down into the sea,

Yet today as of old, the red ring of dawn flares up in the sky.

3

Done is what had to be done, and all ways are completed.

Clearest awakening does not differ from being blind and deaf.

The way he once came has ended under his straw sandals.

No bird sings. Red flowers bloom in glorious splendour.

Picture 9

RETURN TO THE ORIGIN, BACK TO THE SOURCE

Returning to the origin is going back to the source like going up a river to its beginning. But in our picture, it denotes even going back to before the beginning. The text says that there it has been pure from the beginning, and there is no dust. Does that not echo the Sixth Patriarch's verse that when there is no dust to settle, in the no-thing-ness, dusting is vain? But pondering carefully, it is not as simple as that. This source or origin is something very special. Someone contemplates the flourishing and withering of that which has no form, contemplates the coming to be and ceasing to be of all forms, including the contemplator himself; such a one dwells, so says the text, collected in the quietness of non-(intentional) doing. The Chinese characters usually translated as non-action or non-doing, 'Wu-Wei', actually a Taoist term, does not mean non-doing in the sense of simply being inactive, sitting and letting the world go by, contemplating the navel, or whatever. Such non-doing gives the wrong connotation. It is rather returning to the origin, to the source, to be re-linked and once more in harmony with all that is. So this particular and crucial term, if we truly ponder it, will yield the right connotations: not non-acting, non-doing in the sense of laziness or callousness — for how could that be the Buddha's Way? — but non-intention, non-interference! In other words, I am no longer there intent on bending things 'my' way.

To be truly at one is to be truly in accord; there is then a natural going with that harmony, acting in accord with situations or circumstances, a natural coming to be and ceasing to be; no struggling against, nor trying to fish out something for me! All forms have their beginning, their existence and their end. Such acting in accord with the situation can be seen as 'non-interfering' — not intentional — and so also means not being a busy-body! When we now look at the basic Buddhist teachings, just this intentional, volitional wanting to wrench things according to some kind of pre-conceived idea or pattern, however good it might seem, is the Karma-producing agency that keeps us bound and revolving on the Wheel. To become free of it is not possible for I, for I am it — picking and choosing being my nature. However, once the Great Death has been died, with the passage through that empty circle, the itch to interfere has also died. Someone who contemplates the flourishing and withering of that which has form dwells in the collected quietness of non-intention.

There is an amusing story about this natural coming to be and ceasing to be, which is one of the three hall-marks of existence, change; the other two being suffering, and No-I. Just because it is amusing, it helps the process of gently disengaging oneself from attachments and from that strong itch to wrench things the way they 'should' be.

In the old days for various reasons little boys were often given into temples and monasteries, brought up there and given a good education; many of them became ordained. This is the story of such a boy who later became a famous Zen master. Like all boys, he was not always good but naughty as well. He heard the various teachings and had picked up some. The temple owned a famous tea bowl, used only for special occasions. One day, not being careful, he dropped and broke it. He was very upset and scared. Then he remembered the teaching of all things coming to be and ceasing to be, and he plucked up courage. His hands with the broken shards behind his back, he came to the teacher, and said, 'I have often heard you say that all things have a beginning and an end?' 'Yes,' said the teacher. 'And is it true that in their season they begin and when their time comes, they cease?' 'Yes,' said the teacher. The boy said, 'Teacher, our tea-bowl's time to cease has arrived,' and presented the broken bowl.

Coming to be and ceasing to be is not an abstract dogma. We can usefully remember this little story when something that is dear to us recedes; if we can smile at it, we are already over the worst of the grief or bitterness or whatever it was that befell us. This is the value of such teaching stories: they help us over a particular hump. Hearing them just once, one forgets them and so it is useful to have a collection and to read through them from time to time. Then, when we are really at point-non-plus or rock bottom, the appropriate story may suddenly arise from the depth of our mind or heart, presenting a new facet; we can then see a way out of the dilemma and can act again.

Returned to the ground and origin; and from there the response to a situation, or to any circumstance, is not an intentional act, but direct, immediate, and appropriate — just right. To an onlooker it may seem to come from we do not know where, and it exacts a response we do not know whose, but it works; nor is it blind impetuosity which always overshoots and at best merely bungles.

Once through that empty circle and back to the origin, he is no longer tricked by the transitory images of the world. Such a being does not stand in need of any further training. 'Blue flows the stream, green range the mountains' is a typical expression of this. What does it mean? For a moment they may even be perceived as just that, but soon, 'I wish the water would run a little faster, it could then have trout in. And wouldn't it be nice if the tree line there could be just a bit higher, then the mountain might look more beautiful. Or if the mountains were but snow-capped — that lovely mountain air . . .' We cannot leave things as they are for long, can we? Intentional interference, picture making, picking and choosing, that is our side here, divorced from our ground and origin.

The text to Picture 9 also says, 'Red flowers bloom in glorious splendour but no bird sings.' It is really back to the origin, back to the source, where there is everything in potential, not yet 'out'. We need to become aware of, and be relinked to this potential from which everything comes, because it is also the source of all true goodness, of all true creativity, of all that which I, in my best moments, long for, but can never 'be'. I cannot be entirely good even if I try; I can but train myself to be reasonably good. Yet this is at best only assumed, is never the real goodness, for the very nature itself is not yet good. This is why when circumstances go really hard, the assumed goodness changes; it is not good in its entire nature, it is only assumed like a cloak that can slide off and often does. But when the nature itself is changed, such a being no longer intentionally interferes, is incapable of any I-intention because I is not there any more, and even wanting to be good has ceased. Here at Picture 9, in the origin everything is pure; now the nature itself is incapable of being anything else but good, in the best human sense.

Therefore, under all circumstances, good, bad or indifferent, even if driven to the uttermost, it will remain good because it is incapable of being otherwise. A mouse will predictably act as a mouse under all circumstances, and an elephant will act and behave as an elephant; an ant will be an ant. But a human being? We are transmigrating through all the six states daily, hourly, even faster — are we not? That is why, although we have human bodies, we are not yet human beings. Our nature is not yet 'human' and so we need to be humanised.

This process of humanisation was completed in Picture 6. In Picture 9, Returned to the Ground and Origin, a further step or change occurs in human nature, for Picture 10 portrays not just a full human being, but a fully completed, spiritual human being — human not only in form as we deluded beings are, but surpassing even the whole human being. This is the greatest development that the human spirit is capable of conceiving — true goodness, which cannot but be good; true creativity which flows and acts in accord with the spirit and itself, and, together with the true warmth of the liberated human heart, manifests in whatever is being done, or shines through it — whether rinsing a cup or in the sculpture of a great artist. Because it is not an artifical or intentional picking and choosing, nor conceived intellectually only, not deceived by the object nor bent by attachment to result, creativity now has free play, and can unfold itself rather than being limited to 'my' delusory expression of it! To this free play belongs then its expression or action, but we will come back to that in Picture 10.

Blue flow the streams, green rise the mountains; the man sits by himself and contemplates the changing of all things. We must not mistakenly take this sitting by himself as somewhere on a mountain peak, looking down from its height at all that beehive activity that goes on below, and contemplating its changing! When there is no longer any separateness — and there is none in the source and origin — there is also a natural taking part, a 'partaking' in what is, yet without being swept away by it. 'To cry, but not to be carried away by tears; to laugh, but not to be carried away by laughter.' True, the Buddha's teaching shows the way out of suffering and I may undertake it because I want to get rid of all my troubles and problems — but actually, that is not how the Way goes. It does, however, get me beyond wallowing in 'my' suffering, which is the habit of I. Far from losing touch with a full humanity, in Picture 9 is the origin, the very source of humanity and of all that is — and of which all of us are part. From there and only from there is the transit to Picture 10 possible.

We must never forget, however, that these last pictures are pointers only, not meant to be understood, not to be taken literally, but pointing at what to me will ever remain a mystery. As that to be revered and be moved by, thus being made receptive to perceive the wonder of life not just as an onlooker but as a participant. A new life!

X — ENTERING THE MARKET-PLACE
WITH BLISS-BESTOWING HANDS

The brush-wood gate is firmly shut and neither sage nor Buddha can see him. He has deeply buried his light and permits himself to differ from the well-established ways of the old masters. Carrying a gourd, he enters the market; twirling his staff, he returns home. He frequents wine-shops and fish-stalls to make the drunkards open their eyes and awaken to themselves.

POEMS

1

Bare-chested and bare-footed he enters the market,

Face streaked with dust and head covered with ashes,

But a mighty laugh spreads from cheek to cheek.

Without troubling himself to work miracles, suddenly dead
trees break into bloom.

2

In friendly fashion this fellow comes from a foreign race,

With features like those of a horse, or again like a donkey.

But on shaking his iron staff, all of a sudden

All gates and doors spring wide open for him.

3

From out of his sleeve the iron rod flies right into the face.

With a great laugh spread all over his face,

He talks Mongolian, or speaks in Chinese.

Wide open the palace gates to the one who on meeting himself
yet remains unknown.

Picture 10

ENTERING THE MARKET-PLACE
WITH BLISS-BESTOWING HANDS

'Entering the Market-place with Bliss-Bestowing Hands' is the usual translation of the caption to Picture 10. Look at this being, 'coming from a foreign race', as the text says. He certainly looks different, does he not?

These pictures are carefully drawn. First of all here he meets another pilgrim who is just about to set out on his pilgrimage, a little chap who looks remarkably like the herdsman in Picture 1. He carries a bundle, and he chances to meet such a Great Being. They talk a while and after that talk he has managed to lay down his bundle and sets out on his quest, as portrayed in Picture 1. Thus seriously started he has not got the bundle any more — of I, me, mine only — though he is still in a split state. They meet, Pictures 1 and 10 — the same yet not the same. So the new aspirant encounters one who has gone before — or conversely, such a meeting may touch off the aspiration to set out on the quest. Either way, it is now the quest that is paramount — no longer 'I'.

This Great Being has a stout staff on which he carries a huge sack with all kinds of goodies. These cannot be seen, only the sack. Nor do we know how heavy that sack is or how light. He also carries a little basket. Is it perhaps like that calabash of the heavenly maiden which, because empty and containing nothing at all, is the source of happiness and abundance? Looked at with impious eyes, 'seeing nothing', the mystery of happiness and good fortune departs. If it is 'nothing but', we have passed by blindly, without seeing! Not seeing what there actually is, we only see what meets the eye! Missing the wood, we get lost among the trees!

On encountering such a Great Being, we may try to imitate him; or we may think, 'Oh look, that is what it is all about. Look at him — all the things that he is not supposed to do, he does them all. He no longer cares about the precepts. That is really what the whole thing is about; freedom — complete freedom! Look at him! Not only has he grown his hair, he does not shave at all; look at his beard! Instead of being decently dressed, he is shabby. If that is meant to be a robe, it is all gaping open and sloppy. True, he does not look special, but see yourself, he shows he is beyond all, beyond good and bad — the great fling, the fine gesture.' That is the mistake we can make — and have made — when looking at such pictures, reading such texts.

But what is actually shown by his being portrayed like that? We are in the province of eastern culture. Little boys in Japan are warned again and again, 'If you have your navel exposed, the thunder-god will come and pluck it out!' That means not just plain death, but utter perdition, and is deeply ingrained. Hence also the cummerbund or belly-band that all Japanese men wear or used to wear; no one would dream of taking it off, even on the hottest day.

So this Great Being in Picture 10, who looks almost indecently exposed to us, actually shows — and that is what is portrayed — the fearlessness of the Bodhisattva, who has just emerged or 'come forth' from the source and origin. What we naturally associate with the Bodhisattva, for such is this Great

Being, is compassion. Hence we would expect the first gesture of a 'new' Bodhisattva to be that of compassion — but iconographically he is always portrayed in the gesture of fearlessness. Real compassion is not possible in the presence of the picking and choosing I. Fearlessness equals I-lessness and that equals Bodhisattvahood.

In the 'Zen Teachings of Rinzai' there is a description of what a liberated being can do — culminating in playing about in the three deepest hells as if in a fairground. When I first came across it, I was upset about the lack of compassion and very curious how Sesso Roshi would comment on this in his Teisho. He took it up, saying that if one looks at such texts in the ordinary way, with one's ordinary judgements, such statements seem callous, but this is where our misunderstanding comes in. We judge far too quickly, without looking, without thinking, without knowing. That is our particular failing, and for that reason, we have so many quarrels with each other.

'He can go into those three desperate, deepest hells and play about as if in a fairground.' What does this truly mean? If a newly fledged Bodhisattva goes into those hells, and sees their extreme misery, what happens? Unless he is completely free, he gets himself caught in that suffering. How as an ordinary human being could one possibly see such misery and not feel, 'How terrible!'? But at that moment he is caught, and just becomes one more inmate.

Sesso Roshi stressed that in a way it serves him right to become another inmate because nobody asked him to go in there. But sadly, by rushing in unasked to become another inmate, he has only increased the sum of suffering by that one. Since that is not the conduct of a Bodhisattva, he had much better not go in at all, unless he is sure that he will not be caught. He must remain totally free, even amid the greatest suffering; for if he does not, how then can he reach out a helping hand to those suffering inmates to lead them out?

This comment of Sesso Roshi impressed me deeply, and has remained with me ever since. The older I have become in the training, the more it has taken on meaning, and no doubt will continue to do so; the deeper into the training, the more meaning it is going to take on. Can we perhaps ponder this, and ponder again and again, before we too quickly interfere once more in the running of the world as we think it had better be?

Coming back to the one with the bliss-bestowing hands, the text also says that he is laughing; and without troubling himself to perform miracles or wonders, suddenly the withered trees break into bloom.

Sesso Roshi, I was told, at a convention of Zen teachers in the late nineteen-fifties, was asked his views on the propagation of Zen. The consensus supported change, more lecturing to the public, perhaps being less severe. Sesso Roshi is said to have commented that he had carefully considered all that had been suggested and he did not believe it to cause any actual harm; but neither did he see what good it could do. Things change anyway with time. Even if more talks and lectures were being given, however eloquent, they would soon be forgotten.

So he thought that the onus would be rather on the would-be propagators. They first should once more really and totally clean themselves out, so that there was nothing at all left, not wanting anything, not even wanting to propagate Zen! If all inside is clean and empty, then so much warmth springs up in the human heart that it overflows. Since all beings also have that same human heart, however little aware of it they may be, coming in contact with such a flowing heart, words are not really necessary. There is that ambience, and the one who has come in contact with it is stirred. He does not know how or why, but a first aspiration arises and prompts, 'I don't know who he is, I don't know what it is, but there is something;' and striving after, starts the training. This is what Picture 10 points at, the function or free activity of a Bodhisattva.

In the beginning our text says that there is something for Buddhas to do, and something for us human beings to learn or carry out. It is also said that in the treadless, the path comes to an end; but it does not come to an end by fizzling out! One of the most beautiful Buddhist parables in the southern teachings is the Parable of the Raft. The Buddha likens his teaching to a raft for crossing a river; once safely crossed over, would the raft then be carried along? No — the answer, as we all know, is that there is no need to carry that raft further; it has served its purpose of carrying over.

We do not think any further, keen only to cross that river as quickly as possible and leave behind what we do not fancy. Then, as I fondly but mistakenly imagine, I am free to disport myself any way I like, without let or hindrance, and so of course will leave that raft behind. Give it a kick — as it is not needed any more, I can demonstrate my freedom! But such feelings or actions merely prove that as yet I am still sitting on this side, and have not even built a raft that carries to the yonder shore!

So it might be taken that once that river has been crossed, once the empty circle has been traversed back into the origin, into the nature of the other shore, then the path comes to an end. The Great Being then returns, but the raft is no longer there. He has himself become a raft to help others across. This is why he is no longer just a human being, but a Great Being, a Bodhisattva. He is available to everybody and everything, and that is his 'work'. Hence it is also said that whatever is touched by him, blooms. He is without any intentions, does not invite, 'Come here, please, I know the way. I am the raft to ferry you along. Just step on, let me pull you!' However well meant, we have to be very careful of zealous intention which amounts to interference. What is truly ripe falls naturally from the tree. Fruit that is not ripe is better not plucked because, gobbled green, it results in stomach-ache. We are all willing, if not determined, to make others conform to our ways and opinions! That is interference.

In contrast to this attitude is Master Issan's, who under threat of death did not rob Kyogen of finding out for himself (see Picture 8). Unless we find out for ourselves by our own training, by our own labour, we will not understand. When it then comes to the point where we are really confronted with the hump, we will not be able to take it. So we must be allowed to do the journey step by step. Easy or bitter, walk on our own feet all the way until we face that empty circle. Otherwise it will go wrong, and we will not be able to traverse smoothly. This is where the true compassion comes in, and we must not forget it. The Great Being knows this, and has the great compassion as well as the great wisdom! Without any intention, he is just there! He will not — doctrinally it is said that he cannot — bring another to enlightenment, nor can Buddha himself, for 'even Buddhas do but point the way'! His being there is his helping; not his to smooth the proverbially hard training, thus robbing the trainee of his own discoveries and insight.

So he is rather like the sun — it shines, for that is its nature. Clouds do not diminish the sun's shining, they only obscure it from us, the beholders. The clouds of our own ignorance usually cover not just the sun, but also the moon. The sun is unconcerned — it just shines, nor does it say, 'Come out and enjoy me!' Only 'I' can feel like that. The sun just shines — it cannot do anything else. How we react to that sunshine, whether we find it too hot and look for shade or whether we bask in it, is up to us. As far as the sun is concerned, our reactions do not touch it, but somehow in a strange way, flowers and plants, too, turn towards the sun. You can turn pot-plants round, but within a few hours they have turned 'of themselves' back towards the sun.

So the Great Being does not interfere with anything. He just goes with his broad smile, with his big sack, and with the precious basket containing the mystery, with the lid carefully closed. Whatever is around him starts suddenly blooming. We, being of the stature of the little lad in the picture, starting the long journey with a beginner's heart, we hope — actually we can be sure — that as our training continues, we will meet such a Great Being, however fleetingly, and from that encounter be 'moved', inspired to take the next step and the next.

My load seems to me oppressive, but is actually quite small and insignificant as the picture shows. As I become aware of 'my' bundle shrinking to its proper proportions, and so of the lightening of 'my' load, I now begin to look around with eyes shining with gratitude at that wonder. A little of the sunshine, and of the warmth of the Great Being has at that encounter penetrated into our heart. And with the heart ever more unfolding and opening up in the process of training, the walking is no longer so difficult, nor the laying down quite so bitter.

To me, the Great Being to which Picture 10 points, is and will remain, a mystery. My sphere of perception is the little lad at the point of going forth, when the first aspiration arises in the heart. That is the needful encounter — for those 'whose eyes are but little covered with dust'. So we can set out on the greatest endeavour, 'In this fathom long body' as the Buddha said, to discover the way all things really are — including ourselves!

CONCLUSION

So our picture series has come to an end, or rather has ended in a circle and new beginning — seemingly, seen from this side. But from the yonder shore — which is right here and now, and yet is nowhere — there is no beginning and no end, no beings to be assisted. The very intention to do so is egotistic arrogance! There is the training, the walking of the Way, the Mountain Peak, and the Empty Circle — and then, in the trackless, the Path has come to an end. How so? See Picture 10. As we bow, reverently, the strength unfolds that keeps us walking.

These and similar pictures have been inspirations and guides for generations of trainees. In their basic message they are trans-cultural and so of import to all desirous of setting out on the great endeavour, the 'journey within'. Thus these pictures might be seen as specially helpful to modern, late 20th century Westerners. Having lost contact with our pyschological substrata, and consequently living, as it were from the head only, unaware of being manoeuvred by the bull within, we are deeply split and so perilously close to catastrophe — variously pictured; but whether seen as nuclear devastation, environmental pollution, aggression from the 'other side' and so on, common to all, and very real, is the concomitant fear. Yet the more I fear something and try to avert it, the more power it gains over me! So much so that is can become a real concrete danger.

Perhaps the message for our time might be to look for the traces of the bull within, to catch and gentle him, so that the strength derived from the transformation of his devastating elemental power may warm our hearts and enlighten our minds. We may thus at long last awaken to the awareness of being an integral part of what is. Re-linked or related once more, delivered from the fear of being 'alone' against all the odds, we may, by working in accord with rather than against it, harmoniously partake in the miracle of LIFE, which, itself BEING, yet is not static but ever growing and unfolding. In the awareness of a Great being, BEING beholds itself.

Inherent in every human heart is the striving for such an unfolding. As the 'outer world' shrinks and shows ever increasing signs of breaking down under the heedless onslaught of over-population, with the spectres of famine and pestilence rearing their ugly heads, we, having brought all this mess about, might perhaps undertake the greatest adventure of all — turning around and setting out on the inner journey. There we encounter what the pictures portray, and for the sake of all that is, ourselves included, we vow to walk the Path until it ends in the trackless. There to turn around again and 'Return to the Market-Place', but now 'with Bliss-Bestowing Hands'.

FURTHER READING

Discourse of the Inexhaustible Lamp, Torei Enji Zenji, translated by Yoko Okuda, Charles E. Tuttle Co., Inc., Boston, 1996.

The Essentials of Buddhist Philosophy, Junjiro Takakusu, Coronet Books, Philadelphia, 1973.

A First Zen Reader, Trevor Leggett, Charles E. Tuttle Co., Inc., Boston, 1994.

Fundamentals of Mainstream Buddhism, Eric Cheetham, Charles E. Tuttle Co., Inc., Boston, 1994.

Mahayana Buddhism, Paul Williams, Routledge-Kegan Paul, New York, 1989.

The Story of Chinese Zen, Nan Huai-Chin, Thomas Cleary trans., Charles E. Tuttle Co., Inc., Boston, 1995.

The Tiger's Cave and Translations of Other Zen Writings, Trevor Leggett, Charles E. Tuttle Co., Inc., Boston, 1995.

Zen Action-Zen Person, T. P. Kasulis, University of Hawaii Press, Honolulu, 1985.

The Zen Way, The Venerable Myokyo-ni, Charles E. Tuttle Co., Inc., Boston, 1996.

THE AUTHOR

Myokyo-ni (Irmgard Schloegl) was trained at the Daitoku-ji monastery in Japan, where for twelve years she worked under the two successive, now late, masters Sesso Roshi and Sojun Roshi.

In 1977 she founded the Zen Centre at the residence of Christmas Humphreys who on his death in 1983 willed it to the Zen Centre. She was ordained in 1984 as the Venerable Myokyo-ni by Soko Morinaga Roshi, abbot of Daishu-in, who had been head monk of Daitoku-ji monastery during the first two years of her training there. At the same time the premises of the Zen Centre were inaugurated as a training temple under the name of Shobo-an.

THE ZEN CENTRE

The Zen Centre is a registered charity with the object to encourage the practice and study of Zen Buddhism. As that, it offers a structured training programme both at its own premises, and at the Buddhist Society, 58 Eccleston Square, London SW1V IPH. Enquiries in writing should be sent to: The Zen Centre, 58 Marlborough Place, London, NW8 OPL, England.